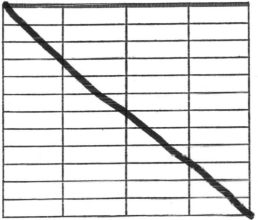

EQUAL EDUCATION

a new national strategy

EQUAL EDUCATION

a new national strategy

John F. Hughes
Anne O. Hughes

Indiana University Press
Bloomington and London

Library of Congress catalog card number: 72-75635
ISBN: 0-253-12350-X

Published in Canada by Fitzhenry & Whiteside Limited,
Don Mills, Ontario
Manufactured in the United States of America

To the Children of ESEA Title I

Foreword

by Senator Walter F. Mondale

It has been my privilege to serve for the past several years as Chairman of the Senate Select Committee on Equal Educational Opportunity. During this time, our Committee has tried to gain an understanding of the extent to which children throughout the country have full opportunity for a quality education, what effect our federal aid to education programs has been having, and how the programs might be improved. We have heard literally hundreds of witnesses—including superintendents, principals, teachers, pupils, representatives of the Office of Education and State Departments of Education, and university professors—testify on subjects ranging from Indian education to school finance.

This has been a challenging, and at times, a very frustrating task. The size of our educational system is staggering—involving nearly 50 million children attending schools in almost 20,000 school districts across the country. Many of these school districts are on the brink of bankruptcy, or are already there. Many of the students—Chicanos, Indians, and other minorities—are confronted with an alien language or an alien culture when they try to learn to read and write. Many of the schools and many of the teachers are forced to operate without the books and other educational equipment they need. And the problems each child and each school district face are often subtly or substantially different from those of the next. In a system of this complexity and this magnitude—where federal aid constitutes less than 7 percent of the total educational budget—it has been difficult to trace the impact of federal programs and make recommendations for their improvement.

Few efforts have helped me identify the impact of federal aid to education programs as well as this book Jack and Anne Hughes have prepared. It contains perhaps the most thorough analysis of our major federal education assistance program—Title I of the Elementary and Secondary Education Act of 1965—produced so far.

And this assessment pulls no punches. It is equally candid about successes and failures. It forces the reader to focus on the mistakes that have been made, however painful that may be. Much to their credit, the authors do not get involved either in scapegoating or in promising simple solutions. Rather than simply blaming teachers or students for the problems that exist, they focus their attention on fundamental and difficult questions including the way we finance our schools and the way we govern them. Rather than simply pretending that more money alone will improve education, they struggle with tough issues such as accountability.

Perhaps most importantly, the authors propose a comprehensive strategy to deal with the problems they discuss. I do not happen to agree with all their recommendations. Some of them are provocative and controversial. Some of them are costly. Some of them may be unrealistic. But all of them speak to the fundamental issues in education that require public attention and public debate.

The American educational system—our system—has made tremendous progress in the recent years in improving the quality of education. But we still have a long way to go before we fully realize the goal of an equal educational opportunity for every child. This book is a very useful reminder of the fundamental issues we must deal with if this right is to be fully realized.

ACKNOWLEDGMENTS

Over the period of two years and three months that this study was in process, the authors benefited from the cooperation of many persons within the Department of Health, Education, and Welfare, of foundation officials and staff, of members of Congress and staff, as well as of general staff support from the Brookings Institution in Washington. The principal work on the study was performed by one of the authors while on a Federal Executive Fellowship at the Brookings Institution and on leave from the U. S. Office of Education. Much of the material used in the study is based on the personal experience of this author in directing the program of Title I of the Elementary and Secondary Education Act during the first four years of its presence on the national education scene (1965–1969). Extensive interviews and field investigations were also used in gathering material for the study and a list of major interviews is contained in the Appendix. Staff members at the Brookings Institution and at the U. S. Office of Education gave generously of their time in providing information and insights to guide the authors in the organization of the study. Particular acknowledgment is given to the assistance of Fordyce W. Luikart, who directed the Brookings Fellowship program of this author during the period from September 1969 to November 1970.

Critical reading of the early manuscript was provided by James E. Mauch, University of Pittsburgh, Alexander J. Plante, Connecticut State Department of Education, and Harold Howe II of the Ford Foundation. Their individual contributions to the anal-

ix

ysis of the ESEA experience contained in Part One of this study are gratefully acknowledged.

Thomas S. Oliver of The Federal City College was a most helpful and painstaking editor and critic of both the original and final manuscripts, and we pay special tribute to his valuable assistance.

Secretarial assistance for the study was rendered most pleasantly and efficiently first by Mrs. Paula Brown of the Brookings Institution and finally by Mrs. Edith De Santis, who skillfully prepared the final manuscript for publication.

The authors accept full responsibility for the views expressed in the study. And, needless to say, neither the Brookings Institution nor the authors' emloyers—the Department of Health, Education, and Welfare and The Federal City College—share in this responsibility.

JOHN F. HUGHES
ANNE O. HUGHES

CONTENTS

EQUAL EDUCATION
a new national strategy

PART ONE
Two Partial Strategies of the 1960's

1

Perspective
and Purpose

PUBLIC EDUCATION ENTERED THE SIXTIES with a comfortable political mythology about its programs and its governance. In only one
area was a problem acknowledged—its eroding fiscal resources.
This problem received national recognition in a short-lived priority in the mid-1960's when the main emphasis was on funding the
system and supporting the mythology. Along with this priority for
educational funding came another one: overcoming poverty and
discrimination, for which an "opportunity" strategy was devised
at the national level. Both priorities became intertwined in the
ensuing federal legislation through Title I of the Elementary and
Secondary Education Act of 1965. The subsequent stormy course
through which Title I of the act traveled as it sought to provide
special assistance for the children of low-income families, using
the schools as the vehicle, revealed that the fiscal problem facing
public education was not its only one. As the remainder of the
decade unfolded, the political mythology surrounding programs
and governance was, in succession, questioned, challenged, and
largely discredited while the problem of fiscal resources escalated
from difficult to catastrophic. By the close of the sixties, public
education was finally peering into the reality of being a social
institution variously under fire from its clients, local taxpayers,
the courts, and governing bodies at all levels.

Now, with the seventies well under way, public education
faces an increasingly harsh reality compounded of fiscal brinks-

5

manship, pressures for institutional reform, a lingering mythology without credibility, dissatisfied clients and taxpayers, and an absence of a well-designed strategy for the needed rescue operation. The limited priority and strategy that emerged in the mid-1960's can no longer suffice for the required rescue operation that must occur in the 1970's. Education has become a national need in search of a continuing priority and a full-fledged strategy. The priority and strategy for the 1970's and beyond must accomplish the necessary reforms in finance, governance, and programs to regenerate the schools as accountable social institutions in order to guarantee a genuinely equal educational opportunity to every American citizen. To settle for a lesser vision is to default our citizens now and our nation in the future.

In bringing this reality to the fore at the beginning of the seventies, the experience with Title I of the Elementary and Secondary Education Act has contributed significantly, not only because of the depth of the problems it has illuminated but also because of the indicators it has offered for solutions. If its $1 billion plus annual funding has been far below the combined state-local expenditures for education, Title I has nevertheless been big enough to reach into all of the states and into virtually all of the nation's school districts. In so doing, its focus upon the commonality as well as the depth of the problems involved has shown that solutions must be generated at the national level rather than at the state or local level.

Such solutions must directly address the areas of program, finance, and governance of public education in ways that aim at its full revitalization. Improvements aimed at only one area or at aspects within an area are never going to succeed. To achieve renewal will require a deliberately planned departure from the historical perspective which has resulted in such views as characterizing education as a privilege, using the Constitutional hiatus as justification for maintaining obsolete financing and governing arrangements, and being satisfied that the provision of access to some kind of education is sufficient. For a departure of this magnitude, the political process at the national level is required; from the national political process must come the definition of priority and the design of a strategy for education in the 1970's and beyond.

That is what this book is—the definition of the priority and the statement of proposals for a new national strategy for education that will effect the revitalization of American public education in behalf of its clients and the nation as a whole. The national experience with Title I of the Elementary and Secondary Education Act constitutes the principal basis for defining this priority and developing the proposals for a strategy. Other programs initiated under that legislation, as well as those programs directly stemming from the opportunity strategy as manifested in the Economic Opportunity Act and the Civil Rights Act, are also considered as they impacted on public education in general and interacted with Title I in particular. In examining that experience and then in proposing a new strategy, the main emphasis is upon the political process as it has taken place within and around education. This process is the key not only to understanding what happened and what was learned but to the successful design and implementation of a new strategy for education as well.

Accordingly, there are two parts to this book, the first of which (chapters 2–7) includes an examination of the national educational experience with special reference to the convergence within Title I of both the opportunity strategy and the limited education strategy of the 1960's. In this examination, attention is specifically directed at those legislative and administrative policies and politics which provide the foundation for the design of a new strategy for education. Chapter 2 deals with the legislative politics of the Elementary and Secondary Act (ESEA), and chapters 3–5 respectively analyze the internal political structures of the federal, state, and local levels of education and how they interacted with each other in the implementation of the strategies of the sixties. In chapter 6 the emergence of the clients as a force in behalf of their own educational advancement and their acquisition of the tactics of advocacy is analyzed. And in chapter 7 a summary of the experience with the prior strategies and an extrapolation of the foundations for a new and full-fledged strategy for education are presented.

In Part Two (chapter 8–10), the design of the proposed national strategy for education is set forth, including its likelihood for gaining political acceptance. Chapter 8 describes the rationale of the proposed educational mandate for the strategy, as well as the formula for funding the educational needs of all of the clients to be served. Chapter 9 describes the key tactics of the strategy at each administrative level in education. And chapter 10 examines the political and administrative requirements essential to the fulfillment of the proposed strategy.

2

Title I and
the Political Process

UNTIL THE MID-1960's, education at the national level had been a priority in search of the legislative pathway that would avoid the morass of the Constitutional church-state and states' rights issues and arrive at the goal of funding both the public and non-public school systems at the same time. After decades of frustration over the efforts to gain congressional acceptance of major federal assistance because of these issues, the rationale and strategy for overcoming poverty in the 1960's provided the breakthrough ingredient needed by the Congress to find the pathway. That ingredient consisted of using the poverty child as the unit for funding the educational system, public and non-public alike. Education's time had arrived in the world of national politics through borrowing from another national priority—overcoming poverty.

Contiguous in time, these two priorities became uneasily and inextricably linked together in Title I of the Elementary and Secondary Education Act (ESEA). Because of this linkage and the size of Title I's funding, the politics that have swirled around Title I have, more than for any other title of the act, contributed to maintaining the visibility of education's demand for a permanent national priority, defining the scope of the priority, and pointing out the requirements for implementing a future national strategy for education. Analysis of the political interplay stemming from the interests of the White House, the Congress, and the education lobbies with regard to Title I is the main focus of this chapter.

Poverty and Education—Priorities in the 1960's

When President Lyndon B. Johnson declared "war on poverty," he sounded the keynote for the decade of the 1960's. With overcoming poverty accorded the top domestic priority, the designers of its philosophy and enabling legislation had to determine the best escape route out of poverty. Two major strategies offered themselves. One was to deal with its consequences or symptoms resulting from the simple lack of money. The essence of the solution here would be a massive, straightforward, across-the-board welfare program. But past experience had shown that welfare programs alone had never produced any marked incentive in or opportunities for their beneficiaries to move up the social-economic ladder to improved lives. Despite this fact, the welfare alternative has great appeal by virtue of its sheer directness, its precedent, and its budgetary specificity. Presumably, it requires only one real resource—money—to solve the problem, and the short-term effects can easily be measured. That is, the ratio of the increased dollar amounts made available to poor people over and above their present incomes provides clear information about the number of people who have crossed the poverty threshold, at least in economic terms.

The other strategy—and a new one of the times—was to deal with the root causes of poverty—the lack of self-realization or, more specifically, the lack of opportunity for self-realization resulting from discrimination and deprivation. Inevitably, this strategy included more than the economic aspect alone. It signaled the necessity for social changes on a broad scale—changes which would involve both personal and institutional attitudes and perceptions, and would require multiple resources. A number of years would be needed before the real effects of this strategy could be assessed with any accuracy. The appeal of the opportunity, or self-realization, strategy is long-term; that is, the one generation up-and-out-from-poverty approach is both more complex and more lasting, but much less spectacular than the welfare approach.

The latter strategy was chosen by Sargent Shriver and his co-designers in 1964 as the one through which to overcome poverty. Within this strategy, education was perceived as a principal vehicle for achieving self-realization for the poor through the opportunities schooling and training could provide.[1] Their high regard for education as a part of the opportunity strategy was, however, equaled by their distrust of the system's capability to serve the clients of poverty. The accruing data on the plight of poor people had made the anti-poverty strategists well aware of the hazards involved in relying on the existing system to deliver relevant educational opportunities to the poor. Also, the Shriver-led forces, quite understandably, would have preferred that the educational component be incorporated directly into the Economic Opportunity Act (EOA), where the community action agencies would control the local use of school funds. Their preference was not realized; education, by this time, was developing into a national priority itself via congressional interest. The prospect of a separate legislative breakthrough in education had swung the Administration to the ESEA route as the favored vehicle for the educational component of the opportunity strategy, although it was not acknowledged as such.

The education priority was not burdened with lofty aspirations. Rather, it represented the culmination of a long legislative effort, strewn with discarded and defeated bills, to find a mechanism through which to fund the elementary and secondary school system in a general way. Traditional school administrators wanted financial aid without the contingencies of major changes either in their programs or in their decision-making process. And congressional momentum, principally sparked by the efforts of Senator Wayne Morse and Representative Carl Perkins, had been growing steadily since the passage of the National Defense Education Act (NDEA) in 1958, followed by the heated campaign of 1960, in which aid to education was a prominent issue. Thus, the search was on in the legislative committees for a new categorical program that would build on the progress of the NDEA and would skirt the Constitutional roadblocks that had shut off previous attempts to find a route to general funding of the educational system.

A new approach was discovered wrapped in an old problem. Poverty and its children led the Congress and the Administration strategists in DHEW and USOE to the design of the "child benefit" theory, which satisfied both the rationale of major new funding for the system and the goal of reaching out to the newly rediscovered children of poverty. Political priorities and legislative strategy combined in 1965 to produce ESEA Title I, but the problems of conflicting assumptions over funding the system versus extending opportunities to people were not resolved in the process. At the time of its passage, the triumph was Title I's formula funding for the system and its money rather than its social change potential for the schools in behalf of a special group of clients. Indeed, the formula and the money—$1 billion the first year—were so overwhelming to all parties to the legislative process that the need for a clear strategy that would define Title I's ambivalent statement of mission in the legislation (see appendix A) was not addressed.

In fact, with the passage of ESEA, the political coalition composed of the President, the Congress, and the education lobbies assumed that the Title I mission had been defined—aid for the educational system using the educationally deprived child as the funding vehicle. However, in a comparatively short period of time, this particular definition of Title I's mission would be challenged and the coalition itself would become fragmented. Beginning with the White House involvement in the early years, the national politics of ESEA Title I is examined.

Lyndon B. Johnson—The Education President

Capitalizing on the success of the 1964 enactments of the Civil Rights Act (CRA) and the Economic Opportunity Act (EOA) as well as legislative initiative in education on Capitol Hill, President Johnson sent his historic Elementary and Secondary Education Bill to the Congress in January 1965. Its speedy enactment, followed by the Higher Education Act of 1965, prompted him to remark that in one year the Congress "did more for the wonderful cause of education in America than all the previous 176 regular sessions of Congress did, put together."[2] And the first year of ESEA was characterized by presidential enthusiasm, haste, and optimism. With typical LBJ fervor in the space of one week in April, following the Senate action, he underscored the significance of ESEA and particularly the urgency for its implementation with such statements as:

> Congress has taken the most significant step of this century to provide widespread help to all of America's schoolchildren. . . . I am proud of what the Congress has done in the last 15 months, since I have been President, to help put education at the top of America's agenda.[3]

And, in Johnson City, two days later:

> First, I do not wish to delay by a single day the program to strengthen this Nation's elementary and secondary schools. I devoutly hope that my sense of urgency will be communicated to Secretary Celebreze, Commissioner Keppel, and the other educational officers throughout the country who will be responsible for carrying out this program.[4]

And, at the White House, after another two days:

> I think Congress has passed the most significant education bill in the history of the Congress. We have made a new commitment to quality and to equality in the education of our young people. . . . Now this is just the beginning of America's first education bill.[5]

Having gained passage of the bill, he then took a personal hand in prodding the Congress to provide—at least for the first year— full funding of the formula contained in ESEA Title I. When Congressman John E. Fogarty of Rhode Island, Chairman of the House Subcommittee on Appropriations, wrote into the appropriation bill the language that permitted all districts to spend the full amounts of their first-year entitlement (although the appropriation bill actually carried only 75 per cent of the required cash), Johnson went along with the "open-ended" language despite his own strong congressional-bred conservatism on federal spending. At the signing of the funds measure on September 23, 1965, he reiterated the urgent need for action to the school people of the nation:

> Today, we reach out to 5½ million children held behind their more fortunate schoolmates by the dragging anchor of poverty. Act now. Get your plans made. Open your schools to the promise of these new programs. I hope that not a single day will be lost. For in education the time we waste today can mean a life wasted tomorrow.[6]

In line with his own call to action, Mr. Johnson spurred Commissioner Keppel to activate the historic program at flank speed and to reorganize the U. S. Office of Education (USOE) in order to achieve this activation. Responding to this presidential zeal, USOE issued guidelines on Title I which prominently conveyed this call to action to the schoolmen of the nation. Also, in line with the President's urging, the federal-state-local spending machinery moved into high gear during late 1965 and early 1966, and it produced a response of welcome surprise at the local school level.

But the euphoria surrounding ESEA's beginning was to prove short-lived. The Johnson budget for fiscal year 1967, released in January 1966, contained only a modest increase in Title I funding (about 10 per cent) and only three-fourths of the amount authorized. Increased defense spending for Vietnam was emerging as a critical priority. Then, in March 1966, the first formal report from the newly appointed National Advisory Council on the Education of Disadvantaged Children, mandated by Title I, alerted the President and the Congress to the difficulties that the schools were having in the first hectic months of implementation, as well as to their progress. The council warned that in addition to administrative problems and personnel shortages, the schools were not doing an effective job of reaching and helping the most deprived children among the poor. Specifically, the council warned that Title I could miss its target.[7]

In a twofold effort to prevent the slippage of the education priority and to deal with the special needs of poverty children, Commissioner Harold Howe II (who had succeeded Commissioner Keppel) convinced the President to call for a national conference in Washington on the education of disadvantaged children to examine the progress of the program. Vice President Hubert Humphrey keynoted the July conference at the Mayflower Hotel with a rousing speech on the significance of the Title I effort. On the following day, with Senator Morse and Congressman Perkins at his side, President Johnson, in his typical impromptu format, assured the conference of his deep personal interest in the Title I program and shared with them some delightful anecdotes of how he convinced his Texas Baptist friends that its enactment was not the signal for a new holy war over the church-state issue. However, at this conference, it also became apparent that all was not presidential roses for the schools. Because of federal budget problems resulting from defense spending, he sternly warned the assemblage that doubling the education budget was not only impractical but highly unwise. "Your President," he said, "must ask his advisors whether a sudden large increase of funds makes good sense in educational terms. Their answer is that waste and mismanagement would bring discredit to the program."[8] Although delivered to the Mayflower audience, his warning was directly aimed at Morse and Perkins who by now were publicly goading him on his budget priorities. And it was in sharp contrast to statements uttered only 15 months before on the day of congressional passage of ESEA, such as: "I don't know of another single piece of legislation that will help so many for so little cost. For every one of the billion dollars that we spend on this program will come back tenfold as school dropouts change to school graduates."[9] Education was definitely fading in presidential popularity, as was the political coalition that had achieved ESEA.

The President's warning also signaled the demise of "full funding" of the Title I formula for the years to follow. He had already placed his own favored program on short rations. And, indeed, Title I was to remain on a declining diet for the rest of his Administration. In a December 1967 visit to the LBJ ranch, DHEW

Secretary John Gardner appealed to the President for more funds for education, including Title I, in the pending fiscal year 1969 budget. But the President would only give assurances of all the money that Gardner might ask for education when the Vietnam War was over rather than relent on his tight 1969 budget ceiling.[10] By now, Gardner realized that the President was "in a box" on his budget and that education as a national priority had lost its momentum.[11] A month later he left his cabinet post to a successor, Wilbur Cohen, who was destined to repeat Gardner's frustrating efforts to convince the President that the education priority should be at least partially restored. In one of his final efforts before leaving as DHEW Secretary, Cohen pleaded with the President to increase his last budget request to the Congress (FY 1970) by another $250 million for Title I to show special presidential concern for education. To no avail, however, the President was adamant about holding down domestic expenditures, including education, and he declined this last chance to polish his image as the "Education President."

The Congress

The rise and fall of presidential ardor over ESEA was only in part paralleled by the Congress. At the beginning, both the President and the Congress were generally in tandem in viewing education as an important priority. If presidential interest was soon to diminish, that of the Congress would not. In fact, the latter years of the 1960's would see a steadily growing initiative on the part of the Congress with regard to education, and Title I would be its focal point. Most of this initiative would center around the definition of Title I as a program for funding the educational system using the deprived child as the funding unit which, of course, suited the education lobbies and the majority of school personnel. However, as the 1960's drew to a close, the definition of Title I as a program directly intended to assist poverty children would begin to secure increased congressional support, and it would contribute not only to defining Title I's mission but also to sustaining the neglected—and now increasingly controversial—education priority at the national level. Understanding the congressional contribution both to defining Title I and to maintaining the education priority requires a return to the committee activities in 1964.

At this time, the rising education priority was reflected in parallel efforts being conducted by the Congress and the Administration. In the Congress, the initiative was carried by Senator Wayne Morse, Chairman of the Education Subcommittee of the Senate Labor and Public Welfare Committee, and by Congressman Carl E. Perkins, Chairman of the General Subcommittee on Education of the House Education and Labor Committee. Their main focus was on finding a way around the church-state issue that had demolished previous education bills in the Congress. In particular, Senator Morse had become a burr under the Johnson saddle by introducing a bill in February 1964 calling for aid to the schools based on unemployment and welfare statistics. He then held hearings in July 1964 and elicited from the leading Administration witness, Education Commissioner Francis Keppel, a promise that the President would support the Morse approach with a bill the next year. Keppel, alert to the potential for a legislative coup, even promised to expand on the Morse formula.[12] Within the Administration, a presidential task force headed by John Gardner (then president of the Carnegie Corporation) was also assembling proposals for White House review in the emerging elementary and secondary legislative package.[13] Keppel, in addition to his congressional liaison activities, was also heavily involved with this effort. An unprecedented period of congressional–executive branch cooperation was at hand in the arena of education legislation.

Keppel then teamed with DHEW Assistant Secretary Wilbur Cohen to work on various formula approaches that would satisfy congressional needs. As they analyzed these needs, it was evident that what the Congress really wanted was a formula which would (a) direct substantial federal funds to the schools, (b) reflect the incidence of poverty, (c) provide participation for private school children, and (d) bring together the various forces supporting education that frequently cancel each other out in terms of their lobbying effectiveness. Their success in producing the ESEA miracle—Title I—via the "child benefit" concept is well documented as a masterpiece of legislative ingenuity.[14]

By selecting the number of children in the age range from 5 to 17 in all families with income under $2,000 as the formula factor, the Administration found a device that not only would have the magic of favoring the rural South in its fund distribution but would be doing justice to urban inner-city poverty in the North—only the affluent suburbs were disfavored. The final polish to the formula came when the House Committee included an amendment sponsored by Congressman Roman Pucinski of Chicago to include in the formula those children, in families above the $2,000 income level, who were also recipients of Aid for Dependent Children (AFDC) each year. That amendment provided a built-in escalation factor which was important to the large cities, since the welfare-based AFDC caseloads were rapidly mounting.

ESEA was reported out of the House committee on March 8, 1965, and was passed by the House of Representatives on March 26. President Johnson then executed one of his legislative masterpieces by persuading Senator Wayne Morse and the Senate Committee on Labor and Public Welfare to report the House-passed bill without a single change (not even corrections of drafting errors) so that Senate passage would avoid amendment and a House–Senate conference. Johnson's tactic was designed to avert a second House vote which could give conservative members another chance to delay or dilute the anti-poverty thrust of the bill. The Senate passed the bill on April 9, 1965. From the point of its passage, the new law in terms of its provisions and administrative implementation was the subject of continuing and undiminished congressional interest, and Title I—with its largely congressional origin, its funding level, and its innovative formula which distributed money on a county-by-county basis—inevitably garnered the most interest.

Indeed, this interest began even before ESEA's passage with the official report prepared and filed by the Senate Committee on Labor and Public Welfare on April 6. Although the Senate committee had gone along with the House-passed version of ESEA, it nevertheless was agitated about surrendering its prerogatives as the upper body of the Congress. Accordingly, the Senate Committee staff wrote a lengthy official report designed to "interpret" the substance of the statute as administrative guidance to the President and USOE. In this report, Senate staff members did not disguise their hopes that ESEA Title I would represent the inception of general aid to the schools, and thus "liberal" definitions of the law were encouraged. Liberalizing, in this instance, meant relaxing the requirements in the legislation of such matters as eligible schools and children. Some of these interpretations were destined to plague the federal program administrators in dealing with local officials who, in their eagerness to get Title I projects going, would cite the committee report's "list of allowable projects" as the authority for a marginally eligible one, such as minimal reductions in class size.

If the liberalization of requirements was one tactic that emerged on the programmatic side of the Congress, a parallel tactic developed later on the financial side. Accomplishing the same liberalizing function, this favorite tactic of the staff members to the appropriations committees has been to insert language into the appropriation bills to protect the allocations of selected states. Thus, when the Title I appropriations were restricted beginning with fiscal year 1967, the House and Senate committees included provisos that protected funds destined for southern states from being redistributed to New York and California, where the numbers of AFDC children were rapidly increasing. The first of these provisos, inserted in the fiscal year 1967 appropriation bill, assured all states against receiving less in the second year than they had expended in the first year (FY 1966) and had the undesirable effect of rewarding states, like Florida, which disregarded quality in their drive to spend the liberal first-year money.

Such tactics—the liberalizing of requirements and the protecting of selected state and local fund allocations—illustrate only the lenient aspect of the typical congressional desire to oversee the administration of federal education programs. The other aspect—dealing with the quality of program implementation—usually sur-

faces when glaring evidences of non-compliance with federal requirements are discovered. This second aspect arose when ESEA
supporters in the Congress and in the field were shaken by the
testimony presented to the Senate Committee on Labor and Public
Welfare on June 20, 1969, by representatives of local poverty
groups from the Delta Ministry in Mississippi complaining of the
misuse of Title I funds by local school officials. A convincing case
against the state was made by witnesses from the poor whose
patience with abusive treatment had been exhausted. These
charges prompted USOE to investigate the state's program during
July and August 1969[15] and to bring about major reforms in the
state practice to ensure that funds, beginning with fiscal year 1970,
were used solely for poor children rather than for the general benefit of Mississippi schools. Subsequently, the Senate committee
report of January 1970 commented on the Mississippi incident
(although not identifying the state by name) and then sternly
warned USOE to step up enforcement of regulations on proper use
of the funds.

> The committee expects the Commissioner to exercise fully his
> authority and responsibility under the law to see that state
> agencies abide by assurances they have given in agreeing to
> administer the Title I funds in keeping with the intent of the
> law.[16]

Thus, a sharp contrast can be found between the committee's
1970 report which veered sharply in the direction of "conform-
ity" with ESEA Title I requirements and its earlier reports which
had encouraged liberal interpretations and had cautioned USOE
against issuing restrictive criteria on project approvals by the
states. This shift in committee attitude reveals a newfound advocacy by the Congress in behalf of Title I as a program directly
aimed at serving poor children. And this attitude is likely to lead
to some new patterns of relationships with the education professions lobbies who have always regarded categorical programs as
basically intended for their professional benefit rather than for
client benefit. Taking a look at the contribution of these lobbies,
who made up the third partner to the ESEA coalition, is essential

to rounding out the analysis of education politics at the national level. As a part of this analysis, a brief overview of the lobbies' principal characteristics and typical modus operandi is given.

The Education Lobbies

Individuals and groups who have pursued the cause of lobbying the Congress in behalf of education legislation have constituted an amorphous army of generals with scattered soldiers and with no fixed battle plan. That part of the special pleading for legislation that fits the formal definition of lobbying is performed by Washington-based representatives of professional organizations, such as the National Education Association (NEA) and the American Federation of Teachers with their large-scale teacher membership, by the smaller organizations representing the special interests of professional groups, like the teachers of deaf children or the librarians, and by the sophisticated equipment and materials suppliers. In general, the lobbies pursue their separate program interests with the Congress and the federal agencies. Only when there is a major funding issue involved have they come together in a coordinated way. They have joined forces in two instances: for the passage of ESEA with its promise of something for everyone and for the Emergency Committee for Full Funding of Education Programs because there has not been enough money for anybody. Both instances have served to keep education visible at the national level.

THE LOBBIES IN SUPPORT OF ESEA

At the time of passage of ESEA, the education lobbies and other organized groups were aligned in support of the bill and their special interests had been considered in the drafting stages. By virtue of the Keppel–Cohen spadework, the major blocs of support for elementary and secondary education, including the key National Catholic Welfare Conference, came together willingly in bringing about the necessary consensus for political success. Old rivalries and a few bloody hatchets were hastily buried early in

1965. The organized groups clearly sensed an emerging breakthrough in the legislative egghunt which had embedded within it
that priceless political commodity—something for everyone. With
that commodity attained, however, the united front of organizations which had come together as part of the political coalition in
support of the bill quickly evaporated following its enactment, as
the organizations went their own separate ways in pursuing individual causes of implementation.

The efforts of these organizations to profit from or to serve
ESEA constituted a mixed blessing. On the one hand, the mammoth NEA got the word out early to its locals with brochures
and filmstrips telling how the new Title I funds could be used.
Since much emphasis was given in that publicity to potential
salary raises for teachers and to visions of shining new facilities,
the NEA campaign generated exaggerated expectations in the
field. This effort, while publicizing the existence of Title I, added
to the woes of the limited information resources of the Office of
Education in trying to provide an accurate story about Title I.
Along the same line, elaborate and detailed brochures were distributed by the equipment and materials companies advising
schools on the kinds of programs that could be launched, stress-
ing the relevance of their products, and offering assistance in the
design of projects. Hardware agents, in some instances, were
actively engaged in writing projects for uninformed local school
officials who were overwhelmed by the necessity of sudden
"paperwork" to receive federal funds. On the other hand, a major
source of information and a generally reliable one, consisted of
the responsible educational journals which carried descriptive arti-
cles and interviews which explained the details of the new legislation and how it worked. In fact, some of these became so valuable
that reprints were used by USOE as information guides to states
and local agencies. Also, the annual meetings of various educational organizations gave liberal time and attention to the new
federal programs.

As the programs of ESEA went operational, education industry newsletters to the field and other forms of communication to
the users of educational products helped to generate pressure on

the Congress to extend the programs and to fund them adequately. Industry had become extremely sensitive to changes in the market for educational products, and that sensitivity was heightened by the erratic nature of the first-year bonanza of ESEA business. When funding problems arose, it was industry that responded more efficiently than the professional education channels in terms of both getting the message out to the field and bringing organized political pressure to bear on the Congress. For example, industry representatives could tell their consumers through phone calls and newsletters whom to contact in the Congress and how to put the message across. Cutbacks in ESEA funding, from the start, had political, as well as economic, consequences.

Indeed, it was the funding cutbacks, in combination with the mounting money problems in most school systems, that produced the second instance of the lobbies coming together. The lobbies, by 1968, were discovering that pursuing their separate interests was failing to satisfy their constituencies. Money problems had become a source of deepening dissatisfaction among all school people, and provided the congealing force for united efforts to remedy them. Thus, a new chapter in the politics of education began to unfold primarily with the emergence of Title I funding difficulties, although other programs were involved.

COORDINATION OF THE PROFESSIONAL LOBBIES

The monetary difficulties of Title I and other education programs, which resulted in a new coordinating mechanism for the education lobbies, were not of sudden origin. The problems with funding had been accruing since the summer of 1966. Because of Title I's magnitude and its county-by-county formula, not only were fluctuations in appropriation level immediately visible to all concerned but discrepancies between authorizations and appropriations were highly visible. As these discrepancies increased, so also did the protests from school administrators.

By way of explanation, ESEA Title I, although developing programmatic thrust, has been primarily known as a federal funding program. When USOE announces the annual county-by-county allocation of funds, it has accomplished a major share of its responsibility under the act. The program, at all levels, is extremely sensitive to these dollar allocations. Following the annual appropriation by the Congress, USOE announces the allocation based on (1) the formula amounts *authorized* by statute for each county and state and (2) the formula amounts made available by congressional *appropriation*. Since the act, except for the first year, authorized much higher amounts than were actually appropriated, the spread between these two amounts grew year by year, as follows:

FISCAL YEAR	AUTHORIZED	APPROPRIATED (MILLIONS)	DIFFERENCE
1966	$1,193	$ 959*	$ 134*
1967	1,431	1,053	382
1968	1,902	1,191	711
1969	2,184	1,123	1,061
1970 (budget est.)	2,360	1,226	1,134
1970 (actual)	2,360	1,339	1,021

* Districts were allowed to claim full authorization.

The dilemma of the growing spread between amounts authorized and appropriated, in combination with a congressional cut of funds requested for fiscal year 1969 and the lateness of the appropriations process in relation to the school year, created major unrest among administrators in the field by the spring of 1968. Indignant and disbelieving letters began to pour into USOE and congressional offices. A further source of irritation arose from the fact that the formula for counting eligible children had resulted in an annual increase in the numbers of "eligible" formula children, because of the growing AFDC caseloads. Thus, with a rising pupil count and a relatively fixed or declining total dollar amount appropriated, the amount per eligible child actually available decreased over the four-year period 1966–1969 from $213 to $161. Adding to the irony of the situation facing schoolmen coping with the rising costs of education was the fact that the authorized formula amounts per Title I child were increasing, rather than decreasing, over this same four-year period from $213 to $314. While federal policies called for concentrating the funds on a limited number of children who could be effectively treated, the fiscal facts of life were pushing the schools in the direction of diluting the services to increasing numbers of needy children. Payments per child by 1969 were down to about one-half of the amount anticipated by the formula.

The sting of an unexpected congressional appropriation cut in Title I for fiscal year 1969 brought home to some of the more astute local officials the fact that they were very poorly organized for national political action. One of their number, William Simmons of the Detroit school system, began to move quietly during late 1968 and early 1969 to bring together representation from the federally impacted school districts, the organized school boards association, the large-city school districts, and the well-established Washington-based associations to coalesce their forces for more effective action in the Congress. On April 28, 1969, John Lumley of the NEA, the largest of the education lobbies, called the representatives together in his office. A common meeting ground for all the disparate groups representing education was the fact of "underfunding" of all authorizations. Thus, the consolidating force became the concept of "full funding" of legislative authorizations. The timely availability of Charles Lee (who left the Senate staff following the 1968 defeat of Wayne Morse) assured competent staff leadership for the newly created "Emergency Committee for the Full Funding of Education Programs," which emerged from this session. Distinguished leadership for the committee was provided by Arthur S. Flemming, former DHEW Secretary and now President of Macalester College in Minnesota.

Lee was soon at work on a sure-fire formula containing the following ingredients: (1) identify all education programs which were underfunded and the amounts of underfunding; (2) select those programs which in dollar terms and political sensitivity had the greatest impact for the field of education; (3) devise a strategy for revising the regular annual appropriation bill as it reached the floor of the House and Senate by adding specific amounts to each underfunded program; (4) tie these amounts together in one amendment (rather than several that might be traded against each other) so that a roll-call vote would be required in which members would be forced to show their support of local education programs; (5) line up as many votes as possible in advance by organized contacts of hometown schoolmen to each member of Congress; and (6) find a member of the appropriations committee to introduce this amendment on the floor.

With authorizations for fiscal year 1970 of $8.9 billion on the statute books, education programs were budgeted at only $3.6 billion by outgoing President Johnson, and this budget was subsequently reduced to $3.2 billion by incoming President Nixon. The extent of the total underfunding of all education programs reached the staggering amount of $5.7 billion. The amount of $5.7 billion was obviously too much to ask for in the existing political climate of White House economy pronouncements and congressional voting patterns. The committee therefore had to design a realistic plan for determining (1) how much additional money in excess of the Administration's 1970 budget requests could be reasonably expected from the Congress and (2) which programs had the greatest political potency or weight with the Congress.

In carrying out the political weighting process, a small group of strategists, representing the NEA, the AFL–CIO, and the National School Boards Association, gave consideration to the restoration of prior year funding levels of those elementary and secondary programs that had received the most reliable congressional support (like federal impact aid) and the education industry's backing (like NDEA equipment). Programs in higher education were given second priority in view of congressional irritation at student "campus unrest." A sum of approximately $900 million was pieced together in a "single package" amendment to be introduced by Congressman Charles J. Joelson of New Jersey, and consisted of the following:

APPROPRIATION ITEM	AMOUNT (THOUSANDS)
1. Federal Impact aid	$398,000
2. NDEA* Title III—classroom equipment	110,453
3. Vocational Education grants	131,500
4. Higher Education facilities	33,000
5. NDEA student loans	40,794
6. ESEA Title I—poor children	180,800
TOTAL	$894,547

---

* National Defense Education Act

When the DHEW appropriation bill reached the House floor on July 20, the Joelson trap had been well set. An amendment which would have added funds only for the federally impacted school districts was offered by Republican Congressman Michel of Illinois. The Joelson forces had anticipated this move as a divisive tactic to pick up conservative votes for impact aid and to scuttle the rest of the package. The amendment was voted down by the proponents of the Joelson amendment and many Southerners who had never before voted against the popular "impact" program. When the Joelson amendment was then raised, it passed by a roll-call vote of 293-120. The strategy of a "single package" amendment had held together, and the victory came as the result of a highly organized political effort that defeated the Administration budget forces and scored an unprecedented triumph over the powerful House Committee on Appropriations.

The House gains were not only held in the Senate, but the Full Funding Committee also succeeded in adding more funds to the politically popular impacted aid program as the bill was rushed to completion prior to the Christmas adjournment. The Senate committee on its own engaged in adding other funds—mostly in DHEW health programs—to the point where the budgetary "add-ons" amounted to $1.2 billion. Signs of a presidential veto of the bill and its added funds were hoisted by President Nixon prior to the Senate action on December 20. The political issue had warmed up to a major confrontation between a President determined to show his intent to control federal spending as a means of combating inflation and the congressional liberals, in need of domestic issues, as champions of the cause of education. When the Senate finally presented the DHEW appropriation bill to the President on January 26, he promptly and dramatically vetoed it over national TV on January 28. His victory over the House liberals on January 29 was assured by his masterful TV appearance which mobilized public support behind a potent reason—inflation—which, by now, overshadowed public concern about education.

While he chose inflation as his major issue for achieving the political victory, President Nixon did include in his rationale a concern for the quality of education. He ridiculed the program of impacted aid as an outmoded form of political largesse—which it is—and he also criticized educational programs for the disadvantaged as being ineffective—and he had backing for this from the reports of the NAACP Legal Defense and Educational Fund.[17] Nevertheless, to insure the victory, he showed his own talent for playing "impact aid" politics. On January 29 the President's veto was upheld in the House with the aid of an announcement from House Minority Leader Gerald Ford that the President would be willing to accept an amendment which assured all federal impact districts of at least 95 per cent of their prior year allocations. This move restored 71 conservative votes to the Administration from "impact aid" Congressmen who had previously supported the Joelson amendment.

On February 3 the President sent a new message to the Congress, now preparing a compromise bill, in which he offered to accept $24 million of the $180 million add-on for Title I. The Congress, however, refused to settle for this "trade" of Title I. In its reply to his compromise offer, the House Appropriations Committee reported a new bill which included the additional $180 million for Title I, with reductions totaling $366 million elsewhere in the budget to accommodate the President's insistence on economy. President Nixon's final offers of compromise with the Senate promised $113 million of the $180 million additional Title

I money voted by the Congress in its final bill. It was this bill which was signed by the President on March 5, 1970.

While the veto setback inflicted by the President obscured the progress attained in organizing educators for political action, the gains were sufficient to assure a continuation of the effort on a larger scale. In the first place, the sheer logistics of organizing to influence congressional action had been effectively demonstrated by Charles Lee and other members of the Full Funding Committee. Also, the gut-level concern for the quality and quantity of educational services for children—and, in particular, the poor—was elevated on the national political agenda as a direct consequence of the bargaining on Title I funding.

In less than a month's time from the signing of the 1970 appropriation bill, the newfound political strength of education was again revealed in House action on fiscal year 1971 funds. On April 9, 1970, the House Committee on Appropriations reported out a new and separate bill in advance of the regular DHEW–Labor bill, with excess funds amounting to $310 million over the President's budget. Included in the excess was $161 million of unrequested funds for Title I, bringing the total sum up to $1.5 billion for the fiscal year 1971. On this occasion, the House voted down floor amendments to add more funds to the bill—which passed on April 14—since the Committee on Appropriations had this time done its own political homework of selecting add-on items, and Title I was now the largest slice of the excess pie. In the Senate, extra funds were added to bring the budget excess to $816 million. A House–Senate conference reduced the excess funds to $453 million, with $161 million still intact for Title I, and the bill then passed the Congress on July 28.

Faced once more with a veto issue, the President took the full ten legislative days allotted to him to decide on signature action. He then combined his second veto of educational funds with a similar action on the HUD money bill on August 11, with "inflation and federal spending" as the rationale. This time the education veto was overridden in the House on August 13 by a 289-114 vote, while the HUD override effort fell short by a 216-153 vote. On August 18 the Senate override vote of 77-18 in favor of educa-

tion was recorded. For the first time in the memory of the education community, the Congress had finished its fiscal year
appropriation before the start of the regular school year and with
additional funds. Riding in on the crest of this latest victory was
the $1.5 billion prize for Title I, resulting from congressional
initiative in the political process. The politics of education had
started off in the 1970's with a triumphant bang.

Nevertheless, the bang becomes less impressive when it is
placed in the context of the deepening crisis in education, of
which money is only one element, albeit a major one. As engaged
in by the lobbies, the politics of education has yet to catch up
with and acknowledge all the elements in the crisis. Indeed, the
education lobbies seem unable to do anything but carry forward
into the 1970's the education priority as it was defined in the
middle sixties with increased dollar levels. Their recent unity on
funding is at best a tactical holding action, and not a solution
strategy. In contrast, the other two partners to the political coalition that produced the priority and ESEA in 1965—the White
House and the Congress—no longer seem generally inclined to
view this definition of the education priority as sufficient. That is,
resulting from the interplay around the funding problems and
the gathering thrust of ESEA Title I as a program designed to serve
poor children and youth, the White House and the Congress are
gradually acknowledging that education politics has acquired a
new dimension. Specifically, this new dimension consists of institutional reform and people change, and it is very different from
the 1965 view of ESEA Title I.

If ESEA Title I's mission was initially conceived as a way to
aid the schools with services to poor children as a vehicle, Title
I's impact on the schools would show how generally ill-prepared
and unready they were to serve adequately the needs of poor
children. What few—if any—people realized at the time of ESEA's
passage was that if Title I was to deliver on its mission, the school
establishment would have to change its programs. Painfully and
steadily, the Title I experience has pointed out that: (1) money
alone is not the basic answer to the needs of the schools; (2) for
the poverty child, it is not enough to spruce up the middle-class

curriculum and expect him to emerge in the image of his affluent peer; (3) federal designation of a target population to be served without sufficient leverage on the locally controlled funds is inadequate; and (4) exclusive attention to the identified needs of only one partner to the educative process—the professionals— results, at best, in an incomplete conception of the actual needs. As the other partner to the educative process—the poverty clients and their advocates—gained awareness of and contributed to Title I's developing program thrust, the message of needed institutional reform and people change has gained entry into the politics of education.

Only through careful analyses of the national experience with the educational programs for the poverty groups from various vantage points can a new priority and a new strategy for revitalizing education hope to be achieved. Moreover, such a revitalization will never occur unless general political wisdom is combined with sound educational leadership on a continuing basis. In the 1970's, the challenge for both politics and education is the strategy for revitalizing American education based on the experience of the 1960's as a matter of national need. With this challenge in mind, the remaining chapters of Part One examine that experience with the educational programs for poor children and youth —and principally ESEA Title I—for guidelines to the strategy for the 1970's.

3

Title I and the
National Scene

THE EMERGENCE OF TITLE I OF ESEA as the educational component of the opportunity strategy has largely been forged as a result
of the clashes which have occurred within the educational establishment. Slowly but steadily, the interpretation of Title I's "contradictory" mandate as a program to serve poor and deprived
children, using the schools as the vehicle for providing special
educational and educational-related services, has gained status and
legitimacy. In contrast, the alternative interpretation of Title I
as a program to aid school systems, using the number of deprived
children as the funding mechanism, has been gradually losing
ground. While effective representatives of the poor on the side of
Title I as a child services program have recently emerged,[1] the
main struggles, which are still in progress, for the control and
direction of Title I's mission have been carried out by opposing
forces within the educational establishment at its several administrative levels—federal, state, and local. And if a new and workable national strategy for education is ever to be achieved, it
becomes crucial to analyze the nature of these recurring struggles
which began with the federal-level agency of the establishment,
the U. S. Office of Education (USOE).

As background for the analysis of the struggles at the federal
level, a few terms are described. As used here, the educational
establishment, in its strict sense, consists of the formally constituted administrative agencies at all governmental levels, including their governing boards where these exist and all of their

professional personnel. In its broad sense, the educational establishment also encompasses those business, industry, and special-interest lobbies, as well as those professional organizations, which have various alliances with the administrative agencies. In both senses, the establishment comes through as a huge sprawling bureaucracy noted for its consistency on two counts: (1) its avowal to serve all of its clients equally (or evenly) and (2) its aversion to any external interference with its discharge of that avowed purpose. Insulation of the establishment from its own clientele—its students and their parents—has been accomplished through a "system," the decision-making mechanism, that serves its internal needs while deflecting external influence.

Within its ranks, the establishment functions through a dominant group of professionals, referred to here as the "traditionalists," who serve its interest for survival and expansion. Challenging this dominant group within the establishment is a much smaller group of "change advocates," whose principal purpose is to modify the system to serve the special needs of the poor as a target population within the clientele. Title I provided a major test of the aims and the artillery of these contending groups. In the case of Title I, the ambiguity and the ambivalence contained in its enabling legislation immediately afforded a potent issue—general aid versus categorical aid—for a clash between the tradi tionalists and the advocates within the establishment. Both interpretations of Title I were possible as the law was written,

Beginning with USOE, the agency of the establishment at the federal level, alignments quickly formed over the issue of whether Title I was really general aid for the schools or categorical aid for special services to benefit a target group of poor children. While the traditionalists, who generally ran the affairs of USOE, looked upon Title I as a welcome and major new source for funding the system, a new and unexpectedly tenacious group of advocates emerged as the proponents of Title I as a means for changing the establishment and its schools through serving the needs of deprived children. As the conflict unfolded, it became apparent that Title I was placing a great strain on the educational establishment with regard to its capability to deliver on both purposes

—to serve all of its clients and to keep external interferences to a minimum. In the main, this conflict revolved around the assignments of priorities to achieve the interrelated ESEA missions, the specific administrative tactics to accomplish the Title I mission in its early stages, the policies and guidelines which were developed to interpret the Title I mandate to the other levels of the establishment, and the enforcement of these policies.

Priority Arrangements within USOE

Before the passage of ESEA in 1965, USOE was the rather minor member agency of the educational establishment at the federal level with its priorities in harmony with the main purposes of the rest of the establishment. ESEA had been supported by the educational establishment in its broad sense, and therefore it was not perceived by the establishment as being intended to make fundamental alterations either in its purposes or in its customary ways of conducting business. Indeed, the general idea of ESEA was to work within the existing establishment, rather than outside it as had largely been done with the Economic Opportunity Act and the Civil Rights Act. The fact that ESEA also generally addressed itself to the need to improve the quality of education being offered—thus implying the need for change in current programs and procedures—was not considered to be a serious challenge. In 1965, it was rather confidently assumed that the educational establishment would know how to act effectively and appropriately on the new programs mandated by ESEA as soon as they could be implemented.

When ESEA was passed, the main priority therefore became its implementation. The pervasive confidence expressed in the educational establishment, however, did not extend to its federal member agency. If ESEA was giving USOE a tryout as an agency in the big leagues (those agencies with multi-billion dollar budgets), its existing bureaucracy was viewed as generally ill-equipped to deal with the new programs, not only by Commissioner Francis Keppel but by the White House and the Bureau of the Budget as well. The second priority thus became USOE's reorganization in preparation for implementing ESEA. Another priority, customarily adopted by virtue of the way federal legislation is designed, received scant attention in comparison with those of implementation and reorganization. This neglected priority had to do with substantive program objectives and policies. ESEA, like other federal legislation, had described only the basic dimensions of the new programs possible under its mandates; the exact definition and translation of these dimensions into the form of program objectives, policies, and criteria being given to USOE as the administering agency. Due largely to the relentless pressure being applied by the White House to speed up implementation and to complete the reorganization, the slighting of this priority would leave ESEA without a master strategy for securing the maximum impact on the educational system from the five titles. And its continued slighting would afford a major opening for the change advocates within USOE.

The presidential priorities of ESEA implementation and USOE reorganization were not carried out with equal effectiveness. In the case of reorganization, there was a great deal of re-shuffling of furniture and people after a presidential task force, especially charged with this assignment, submitted its recommendations.[2] The reorganization brought a new administrative chart; some new bureaus, including one named the Bureau of Elementary and Secondary Education, which was assigned Titles I, II, III, and V of ESEA; and an additional title for Commissioner Keppel, Assistant Secretary for Education. While USOE acquired budget approval for some 330 new positions and was given 30 additional supergrades, which provided token increases in its numerical strength, these changes added very little to its position of power either with the other federal agencies or with the educational establishment at the state and local levels.

At the same time reorganization was taking place, individual task forces were created by Keppel's Deputy Commissioner, Henry Loomis, to begin dealing with questions over program priorities and to plan the implementation of each of the ESEA titles. Indeed, implementation of the new titles, rather than their substantive program thrusts, was given an absolute priority over all other assignments in USOE. Traditionalist views prevailed in the priority assignment process for implementing the five titles of ESEA. And at the top of the list were the administrative funds ($25 million), authorized by Title V, to strengthen the leadership of the state educational agencies. Under pressure from the chief state school officers who viewed these funds as their personal slice of "general aid," USOE gave the green light to this title to clear its program instructions with the Bureau of the Budget and to obtain plans from the states which could be quickly processed.

Title III of ESEA, innovative educational centers, was one of the two glamor programs emerging from the Gardner task force report. On the grounds that Title III was the most complex, as well as the most innovative, of the titles to administer, it was given the largest share of USOE staff resources. USOE and particularly the Bureau of Elementary and Secondary Education consistently touted Title III in the hearings before the Congress and elsewhere as the program that would yield the greatest educational return for the federal investment, despite grumbles from traditionalist sources that it was end-running the state chiefs. Title IV of ESEA, research, was the other glamor program of the Gardner task force. Like Title III, this program was given prominence in the congressional hearings for its potential for improving the school system through research and innovation. Assigned to the research bureau in USOE, it was allowed to proceed with its new mandate without reference to the other titles. Its immediate goal was the creation of new research laboratories, and 21 of these were rapidly funded by USOE throughout the country during the first year of ESEA. As it turned out, the creation of "instant" research by this rapid funding process not only failed to support the operating programs of ESEA but also proved so precipitous that the Bureau of the Budget forced a review of all laboratories which resulted in an eventual closing of 11 of them.

Title II of ESEA, funds for books and materials, was given "affectionate" treatment in the publicity area because of its sponsors—the librarians, the publishing industry, and the parochial schools. But it was not given a major slice of USOE resources and, indeed, figured low on the scale of potential impact on the schools.

For its place in the priority setup, Title I of ESEA was assigned top billing in public information because of its funding wallop—$1 billion the first year—but it was given second priority to Title III on staff resources and to Title V on scheduling. Title I's glamor rating was definitely lowered by the absence of a federal approval provision for local projects, and it was assigned, therefore, a lesser share of USOE staff resources and policy limelight. In fact, USOE's priority treatment of Title I reflected a sense of victory at receiving the massive new grant of authority coupled with an anxiety to unload the responsibility for the new funds on the states and the local school districts as expeditiously as possible. At that time, the sheer mechanics of getting Title I operational—in terms of allocating funds by counties, designing forms for project approval, and detailing the provisions of the act—influenced USOE leadership to assign Title I an operational, rather than a substantive, priority over the other ESEA titles. Making the formula work and distributing the funds efficiently became the first concern of USOE.

When it came to USOE organizational arrangements, ESEA Title I was assigned to the new, but traditionally oriented, Bureau of Elementary and Secondary Education. The reorganization plan was concerned with structural tidiness rather than with program mission, and there was no major concern for serving the disadvantaged in the organization theory. The title chosen by the USOE leadership for this new division left no doubt as to the prevailing view of the Title I function—strictly management and accounting—and it was described by USOE to the Congress in the following way:

> *Division of Program Operations.*—This Division would have responsibility with respect to administering grants including compliance with requirements for accounting for the expenditure of federal funds. . . . In addition, it would be responsible for administering . . . payments to state education agencies for grants to local school districts for the education of children from low-income families. . . .[3]

The emergence of Title I as the main educational component of the opportunity strategy with a potential for educational innovation and reform still lay in the future. In the early stages of ESEA's implementation, both the task forces and then the new operating divisions did a highly creditable job of placing the five titles of ESEA into operation. The priority for fast implementation, demanded by President Johnson, had been achieved—ESEA was definitely ready to go in the fall of 1965.

The Emergence of the Change Advocates

As its five initial titles went operational in 1965, the accomplishment of the substantive program priority for ESEA still remained. In the case of Title I, USOE had not yet formulated a strategy for coping with its "special treatment" mandate for a target population of disadvantaged children who had been defined only in statistical terms. In fact, Title I's program mission was already generally assumed by the traditionalists who were advising Keppel on policies to be followed in implementing ESEA. In their opinion, Title I's mission was to assure that the funds flowed as freely and smoothly as possible into the coffers of the nation's school systems with the minimum number of strings attached. In short, Title I—if not quite yet general aid—was to become so in due course. If the "child benefit" theory had been used to sell Title I to the Congress, the idea of specifically serving the target population, as defined in the allocation formula, with special programs to meet special needs was not a major consideration.

In contrast, the advocates in the new Title I unit saw the child benefit theory as the prime focus of the legislation and thus the main basis for developing substantive program policies and requirements which would, of course, restrict the use of the funds. In their opinion, Title I was a categorical aid program intended to serve only the special needs of the poverty target population as defined in the law. From this position, it was comparatively easy for this group, armed with the War on Poverty's accruing data on the plight of deprived children, to arrive at the conclusion that through the development of judicious policies and requirements, the Title I funds could serve not only the specific needs of deprived children but as a change agent within the school systems as well. As ESEA became operational, the advocates in the Title I unit devised several administrative tactics in 1965 and 1966 that directly challenged the traditionalist position on the mission of Title I. These tactics evidenced a marked shift in the thrust of Title I's mission and produced the first clashes with USOE's leadership. The "slighted" priority of program definition would become the focus of major attention.[4]

A TITLE I DEFINITION—THE TARGET AREA

As Title I moved out of the phase of drafting regulations and forms for implementation into the phase of guidelines development, the first signs of the shift away from the traditionalist position began to appear. In the main, these signs consisted of the choice of a new type of staff in the nucleus group that was to direct Title I. These individuals, who represented professional competencies outside the traditional "school administration" group which ruled USOE, turned their attention to Title I's program mandate rather than to its administration. From the outset, this staff began to work on program policies that were designed to turn Title I into a categorical aid program for impoverished children. The struggle over program definition was about to begin, and it would develop into a grim battle against the forces of "general aid."

The idea of general aid had been lingering over the educational scene for almost two decades before Title I's inception, and this idea gained a new lease on life with Title I's enactment. True, the new funds were intended for "deprived children," but to many the "deprived" was anyone subject to an inferior education. Also, the congressional reports and hearings were replete with examples of the permissibility of the use of funds for any activity that served deprived children. The House report even stated that at times the best use of Title I funds would be to improve the level of all the schools in those school districts where poverty was a general condition. Initial contacts with the state educational agencies were by no means reassuring on the question of categorical limitations on the use of funds for poor children. Queries from the states on Title I typically related to the timing and distribution of funds: the permissible use of funds, say, for pent-up construction needs or the logistics of administration. State representatives showed practically no concern for the problems of devising effective treatments for poor children or for reaching the poorest families in the communities.

Thus a first concern of the advocates in the definition struggle was to define the target area in such a way as to limit it to the schools with high concentrations of poor children, that is, those schools serving the "higher than average" number of poor children in the school district. This principle soon ran into trouble in the mountains of West Virginia. When state and local educational agents found that USOE was running a line down the middle of their schools, they protested against using "percentages" as the ranking criterion. Their point was that a large (consolidated) school with a high number of poor children might have a low percentage while a small isolated school might have a low number but a high percentage. So at the insistence of Senator Jennings Randolph from West Virginia, USOE agreed to a change which allowed states to rank their schools on either a percentage average or a straight numerical high and low basis. When this change appeared in the USOE guidelines, those states which were eager to spread the funds told their local districts to use *both* techniques of ranking and to include a school in the target area if it appeared in the upper half of the high concentration on *either* basis—thus spreading funds to more than half of the schools in any particular school district. While the struggle over definitions would continue to gain momentum, the Title I advocates fully realized that the tactic of policy definitions would never accomplish the categorical aid mission. They needed people with whom they could work at the state and local levels, and so another tactic was devised.

CREATING THE STATE TITLE I COORDINATOR

In attempting to find people with whom they could work, the Title I unit had to take on the sticky problem of dealing with the states and their chief state school officers who were almost always strong traditionalists, which meant they were also strong supporters of general aid. Moreover, as the Title I implementation was organized, its policy statements went from Commissioner Keppel to the chiefs. Thus, there was both a "philosophical" and a "procedural" side to the problem. And it was completely evident to the Title I staff that if they were to have any hopes at all for infusing the Title I mandate into the state educational agencies, they had to find a way to circumvent the chiefs.

Proceeding in several phases, the tactic to establish and maintain a contact within the state educational agencies was markedly successful. The first step was for the unit to find a liaison person in the state agency who could be trusted to carry out the mandate. For this purpose, the Title I staff invented the "State Title I Coordinator." The unit began to bombard this mythical figure with letters and bulletins—and always including courtesy copies to the chiefs. The second step was to assure that this individual had a staff to supervise. So a request was made for the state plan of organization with details of positions available to the "Title I unit." As a result, all of the states created both "coordinators" and "Title I units" of varying degrees of administrative power. Rumblings about USOE "empire building" began to come from various chiefs, but the scheme worked. A subsequent ripple effect of the state coordinator creation was that most states asked for the designation of local "coordinators." Third, to find out just what the new state Title I coordinators would be like to work with, the USOE Title I unit hastily went to work to solidify the "merger" by calling five regional meetings to brief the new coordinators on the policy guidelines. It was, of course, not certain who would appear at these meetings, but it was clear that the chiefs were not expected to attend. It was hoped that some vigorous new "administrative types" would come to the meetings identified as the state coordinators, and the batting average on this score was surprisingly high.

The first meeting was held on October 14, 1965, in Atlanta with the southeastern states. This group of states would be by far the most difficult to deal with in terms of educational change. Already deep in the process of compliance problems with Title VI of the Civil Rights Act, these states were in a surly mood, and Alabama led the way. Dr. Austin Meadows, a tough veteran of Alabama's elective processes, was the lone chief state school officer to attend. Arriving early, he took a front seat at the opening session, which he soon interrupted with his own interpretive commentary on the congressional intent, his purpose being to avoid another set of despised federal guidelines. He proceeded to declare his intent to operate the state program on the basis of his own interpretation of the law and thereupon left the meeting. At this same meeting, trouble from Florida was signaled by noisy interruptions at every point by the fiscal officer of the state, who made it plain that he was going to see that Florida spent every nickel that was coming to it and with a minimum regard for federal guidelines—a feat that he did, indeed, accomplish. Otherwise, the state groups showed a lively and serious interest in USOE's guidance and participated constructively.

The Atlanta meeting and the others that followed produced generally the same results. However, the meetings were only partly successful. While they were in progress, the new policy guidelines, aimed in the direction of categorical aid, would be seriously compromised by concessions which the USOE leadership felt it was necessary to make to the conservative leaders among the chiefs, and these are discussed later in this chapter. Nevertheless, the five regional meetings were successful on two counts: They established a new personnel liaison between the federal and state levels, and they demonstrated the acceptance of federal guidelines. In fact, the new coordinators were not only willing to accept the guidelines but they were, in most instances, also eager to have them. Providing special programs for deprived children in school settings was a new task for everyone.

NEW IDENTITY FOR TITLE I—COMPENSATORY EDUCATION

In their efforts to define and implement Title I as a substantive categorical aid program, the USOE Title I group fully recognized the importance of the tactic of using some kind of a "glamor name" which would symbolize its major mission—like Head Start. Despite early labeling efforts, ESEA Title I never had the good fortune to acquire this type of name, and like other USOE programs became known by its "Title" in the statute. Its word title, "Financial Assistance to Local Educational Agencies for the Education of Children of Low-Income Families," was obviously too cumbersome for effective designation of the program, and so USOE and state personnel quickly settled for "Title I" as the program designation. As the largest component of ESEA, its identity quickly spread to the educational community under the Title I designation; so it did become widely known, if not glamorously so.

At the time ESEA was passed, the term "compensatory education" was beginning to appear in the educational literature. Benjamin Bloom of the University of Chicago and others were beginning to define educational services to deprived children under this term. Since much of the descriptive material that USOE was preparing to describe the Title I mandate fitted this new term, the Director of the Division of Program Operations, in the spring of 1966, requested a change in the name of the Title I unit to the "Division of Compensatory Education." When Harold Howe II, who had succeeded Francis Keppel as Commissioner of USOE, placed the proposed name change on the agenda of USOE's Executive Group (now firmly back in the hands of its "traditionalist" forces with the departure of Henry Loomis), the resounding opinion of the group was "no" to the change. That is, all except for Howe. It was clear to the traditionalists that a change in name both implied a new USOE thrust at program leadership for the poor (which they distrusted) and threatened the comfortable idea of passing the money out to the states and their local districts. Howe saw the point of the name change, and it was subsequently approved by then Secretary John Gardner in July of 1966. However, it had taken a full year for USOE to decide, and to declare through an organizational title, that Title I had a substantive purpose—compensatory education for the poor —as contrasted with the "operations" concept of passing out the federal money. But despite the achievements of a unit name signaling program substance, the creation of the new state-level Title I coordinators, and acceptance of the concept of guidance from the federal level through these new coordinators, the Title I advocates were steadily losing ground to the traditionalists in the critical areas of policy definitions and compliance with federal requirements. And it was primarily in these areas that the issue of whether Title I would become general aid or categorical aid would be ultimately settled. Nevertheless, through their initial tactics, the Title I advocates had succeeded in making the issue a real one.

Policies and Guidelines

Only through the development of strong and clear federal policies could the issue of Title I's program mission basically be resolved since its enabling legislation was ambiguous. Such policies were absolutely essential if Title I was to become an effective categorical aid program serving the educational and education-related needs of poor children. Although the underlying issue— general aid versus categorical aid—remained the same, the main conflicts were waged over specific program issues. Two of these issues are discussed as examples: the draft guidelines and the belated development of basic criteria. On each one, USOE would be divided along traditionalist and advocate lines.

DRAFT GUIDELINES

In dealing with the issue of the draft guidelines, it is necessary to return again to the summer of 1965. Early in the inception of planning during that summer, the Title I staff realized that the new programs in the field would require definition of "size, scope and quality" features to be incorporated in local projects. The law itself had called for "basic criteria" to be developed by the commissioner to govern the local projects to be submitted for state approval. However, this provision of Title I, which gave the commissioner some program control over the substance of local projects, had been practically negotiated away by DHEW in its dealings with the Senate Committee on Labor and Public Welfare. In its report, that committee had agreed to allow the House bill to pass through unchanged and had also obtained a further agreement from DHEW that all "basic criteria" would be incorporated in the official regulations governing the program, which would limit them to cumbersome legalisms. Moreover, federal regulations are read by lawyers and not by administrators, who work from guidelines. While the Title I regulations were procedurally very well documented in terms of project area limitations, inclusion of non-public school children in the project, the allocation process, and the project approval process, their utility for local administrative use was very low. Therefore, the staff turned to other means to get across the needed program guidance to the field.

In order to prepare for its five regional meetings, the Title I staff had hastily assembled a draft set of "guidelines" which were to reflect USOE policy in interpreting Title I to the states. Having been embargoed by the Senate Report from a "basic criteria document," the staff hoped to get some strong principles of the new mandate into its program guidelines. At the upper levels of the Bureau of Elementary and Secondary Education, traditionalist heads were suspicious that the intent of the Title I staff was to slip across too much federal control over the states. A tight limit was placed on the number of copies of the draft (only 300) that could be duplicated for the meetings, despite urgent pleas from the states for materials to use with their local districts who by now were impatient to get going.

A key point to get across at each meeting was that dealing with "concentration" of Title I funds on a limited number of children, which USOE was interpreting at that stage as the "formula" number for each state and county. By the end of the first two-day session in Atlanta, this point, along with others, had been carefully explained to the group and most state objections had been answered, although all were not content with the answers. In Dallas, three days later, the problems of target area definition were being discussed with the southwestern and Rocky Mountain states and again the principle of "concentration" was explained to the group. On the evening of the first day of the two-day meeting, the Title I director received an urgent telephone call from the Bureau director, Arthur L. Harris, who relayed the message that Commissioner Keppel was withdrawing the draft concentration principle. Harris stipulated that the principle was to be stricken from the draft guidelines, and the state representatives were to be so advised of its withdrawal. Also, the Title I director was further advised that if he could not follow this directive, he would be relieved of the Title I responsibility. The withdrawal instructions were carried out, and in the ensuing meetings the provision was expunged from the draft guidelines prepared especially for the meetings. The staff limped through the remaining sessions and had the difficult mission of explaining to the new state representatives that a key provision of Title I's new mandate was wide open for state interpretation. The regulatory requirement for "concentration" on a "limited number" of Title I children who might participate in the special programs offered by the schools was to be left to state discretion.

The dispute over guidelines continued during another meeting taking place in Hawaii while the Title I staff was completing its meetings with their new state-level counterparts. At the Hawaii meeting of the Chief State School Officers were Commissioner Keppel, Elementary and Secondary Associate Commissioner Harris, and DHEW Deputy Assistant Secretary Halperin. Negative reactions to the new draft Title I guidelines were forcefully brought to Keppel's attention by conservative leaders of the state chiefs. Still reeling from an encounter in Chicago over Title I (discussed in chapter 4) and the LBJ treatment that accompanied it, Keppel was in a conceding mood and promised the chiefs that the draft guidelines would be "slenderized" by USOE before they were finally issued. At the same meeting, Halperin told them that Title I funds were available for any purpose the states wished to make of them as long as they were used for deprived children, which further compromised the concept of federal guidance in the use of the funds. Harris then invited any states wishing to meet with him back in Washington to send representatives to a meeting on November 23, and necessary changes in the draft Title I guidelines would be negotiated.

At the November 23 meeting with the 15 states who agreed to send representatives, the traditionalist leadership of USOE carried the day. Overriding the protests of representatives Wilson Riles from California and Alexander Plante from Connecticut, the only two states present to advocate strong guidelines in favor of poor children, the majority of the states took an adamant stand in favor of weak guidelines and broad discretion to the state-local complex in the targeting of funds. And one by one the key elements of the Title I restrictions—limited pupil participation, strict project area definition, careful project design and approval, and concentration of services on schools having the highest numbers of poor children—were dissected and weakened under the insistence of state representatives from North Carolina, Tennessee, Montana, and other states who attacked the draft guidelines as an effort at undue federal control and as being inconsistent with earlier USOE positions. Not content with slenderizing—and ten derizing—the draft guidelines, the Bureau of Elementary and Secondary Education leadership went back to the regulations that were already approved and published in the Federal Register and agreed to modify them in order to appease southern states who wanted to stretch the project area concept to include all local schools.

The final guidelines which emerged from USOE in 1966 reflected these concessions to the state pressures and omitted draft guideline language calling upon the states to reject projects which failed to measure up to project area definitions. Clearly conveyed to the states was the impression that Title I was indeed what most of them wanted—general aid—with only mild admonitions to use the funds in behalf of poor children. These political concessions were made despite the warnings of people knowledgeable about

educational efforts with deprived children that minimal or diluted program services to excess numbers of children would be
fruitless. To no avail, Title I as a substantive compensatory education program had sprung a major leak in the dike, and the first
systematic attempt to stem the flow was not made until 1967,
when new guidelines were devised.

BASIC GUIDELINES—FINALLY

By 1967, it was becoming apparent that next to the failure to
fund its formula fully, the failure to implement the basic criteria
provision in the statute during the first two "expansionist" years
of Title I was the most serious flaw in the federal implementation
policy for the program. If the schools continued to be desperately
in need of money to serve their poor and deprived children, they
were also in need of definitions for its effective use. The general
combination of the weak federal guidelines, the laissez-faire administrative style of the states with regard to their local districts,
and the continuation of the same local-level educational programs
with only cosmetic modifications was beginning to yield evidence
that Title I as a program to aid poor children was wide of the
mark. This evidence was accumulating in the reports from the
National Advisory Council on the Education of Disadvantaged
Children, the first round of state evaluations, and the inability of
USOE to discover any genuine Title I "success stories" in response
to demands being made by the Bureau of the Budget, the evalu-
ators within DHEW, and the late Senator Robert F. Kennedy. In
the program area, what the evidence pointed to was that the educational establishment at the state and local levels generally
lacked both the competence and the desire to design effective new
programs for the poor and that federal intervention would be
needed. It was not enough for the Federal Government to "implement," "expedite," and "administer" the provisions of the law,
USOE would finally be required to spell out the precise terms for
using the funds in ways consistent with the Title I mandate.

As the presidential decision to place fiscal restraints on the
third year, and succeeding years, of Title I became evident and

the inadequate educational services for the Title I children surfaced, the Title I staff decided to risk invoking the "basic criteria"
provision in the legislation which would deal with almost all of
the program issues, despite the embargo imposed by the first
Senate committee report. In particular, the staff was convinced
that strong and precise definitions of project areas, pupil participation, priority use of funds, limitations on capital outlay expenditures, and project design features were essential—indeed, they
were overdue.

On April 14, 1967, the first statement of basic criteria was issued
by the Director of the Division of Compensatory Education and
approved by his immediate superior, Associate Commissioner
Nolan Estes. One criterion set limitations on the use of Title I
funds for school construction and equipment—known to be excessive, particularly in the South—to the minimum required to
implement approvable projects, and not to exceed 10 per cent of
total project costs. While the state reaction was generally favorable, the impact of the 10 per cent limitation on the education
industry was another matter. The aftermath of the first- and
second-year bonanza of equipment-buying was settling in as the
schools were shifting away from "hardware" projects to "people"
services.

Donald White, the lobbyist for the National Audio-Visual Association, exploded upon learning of the new criterion and brought
immediate pressure on Howe to rescind it. Knowing that Howe
had strong beliefs about the effective use of Title I, White
brought pressure through the legislative route, invoking his
friendship with the Counsel of the Senate committee, Jack Forsythe, and Charles Lee, via Samuel Halperin, the DHEW legislative liaison. Forsythe and Lee reminded Halperin of the 1965
Senate stipulation limiting the basic criteria provision, and asked
that the new criterion be withdrawn or at least that the offending
10 per cent reference be deleted. Also, a new Deputy Commissioner, Graham Sullivan, had his own strong opinions about the
pressing equipment needs of the schools. He interceded with
Howe and convinced him to soften the new Program Guide. Ten
days later, on April 24, 1967, a clarification of the initial criterion

was sent to the states specifying that the 10 per cent factor was a "guide" and not a fixed limit on capital outlay expenditures. Once more, USOE had shown the wavering nature of its policies, and the effort to secure state compliance with the first set of basic criteria received an early setback.

Nevertheless, in the following year (1968), the criteria were revised and strengthened, and this time they were issued over the signature of Commissioner Howe. Definitions of priorities among the target population were spelled out more precisely than before, and the principle of fiscal comparability between target and non-target schools was enunciated for the first time. Thus, with the support of Commissioner Howe, the Title I advocates had come a long way from the 1965 debacle of the November 23 meeting—Title I now had strong and explicit federal policies. Now the enforcement of these policies would become critical to the success of Title I, and it would afford the next battleground between the contending forces within the educational establishment.

Enforcement of Policies

If USOE had limitations on its policy-making authority and capability—and these have been legion—its ability to enforce its policies has been even more limited. The state agencies and the local districts, by and large, were used to going their own ways, which often meant disregarding federal requirements. In the case of ESEA Title I, practically total reliance was placed on the integrity and capability of the states to live up to their "assurances" to the commissioner. And if USOE had a weak enforcement reputation, that of the states was even weaker. In this context, Title I guidelines and policies were sent to the states, explained to them and cleared in draft form, and then USOE exhortations were relied on for their enforcement. However, the advent of the new basic criteria for Title I, when coupled with the assurances from the states, set the stage for USOE to exert leadership in the area of enforcement. In this connection, USOE was already engaging in activities which lent themselves to enforcement purposes, despite the pervasive "general aid" attitude of much of its leadership and the lack of staff for carrying out such activities. Now the real test would come on whether or not USOE would effectively challenge the concept of reliance on the states, if they failed to live up to their assurances, through either withholding funds or demanding their repayment. The remainder of this section briefly examines the kinds of federal enforcement activities that were carried out by USOE.

DHEW AUDITS

When ESEA was launched in 1965, DHEW asked the Congress for 25 new field auditors to give primary attention to all ESEA activities in the state and local educational complex, but only six of these positions were expected to serve the needs of Title I. While this position request was a modest one in terms of the magnitude of ESEA (specifically, $200,000 to audit $1.3 billion), it was looked upon as a breakthrough to get audit staff at the beginning of a program to exert preventive caution on the state agencies. The Congress was advised that the new staff would permit the auditors to get to the states for audit purposes one year following the expenditure of funds, rather than permitting the habitual two- to three-year lag. The audits did not occur as fast as USOE had hoped, and DHEW had planned. However, when the audit reports did begin to arrive in quantity in 1968, it was evident that the state and local educational establishment was in very hot water fiscally.

Over the years, the states had learned how to argue their way out of fiscal disallowances taken by the DHEW auditors through the simple process of pleading with the USOE Commissioner to have the disallowances "waived." With this history of forgiveness behind them, the state agencies generally did not make any major adjustments of their operations to prepare for DHEW audits during the 1965–1967 period, despite repeated warnings from USOE that these audits would be more searching than previous ones. Thus, when DHEW analyzed the first 15 states audited in a report to USOE early in the spring of 1969, it revealed consistent shortcomings in state fiscal practice. When these findings were analyzed in USOE and relayed to the states in 1969 with a somber analysis of their significance and an alert to reform fiscal practice, the chiefs responded only sporadically to the warning since they had found that USOE could be argued out of any sticky exceptions that might be taken.

However, something happened to the Title I state agency fiscal audits on their way to the USOE files in the spring of 1969. The audits became a major element in a special review of Title I carried out by the "Washington Research Project." The "Project," headed by Mrs. Ruby Martin (now working for the NAACP Legal Defense and Educational Fund, following her resignation as the DHEW civil rights director), used the DHEW audits as the basis of the research into Title I expenditures. She had a field day with the disallowances that were being reported, such as the purchase of a church in Detroit and the construction of swimming pools in Louisiana. Caught between the audit findings and its own negotiations with the states, USOE acknowledged the basic accuracy of the Martin report in a speech by Commissioner James E. Allen, Jr., in Phoenix on November 19, 1969. At that point, the heat was turned on the states through the press and the Congress to mend their fiscal habits. And as a result of the audit disclosures, the demand for enforcement of Title I policies was now suddenly coming via the route of public advocacy (the subject of chapter VI).

In contrast with the DHEW audit and enforcement procedures, USOE's own monitoring activities were designed to identify and then to make recommendations about state problems, rather than to insist upon compliance with federal requirements. These activities would prove to be ill-suited to the new demands for enforcement.

STATE MANAGEMENT REVIEWS

More in the style of USOE operations than the audit reports was an activity termed the State Management Reviews. Initiated by the Bureau of Elementary and Secondary Education under the auspices of Title V of ESEA, these reviews were to look at all state management activities involving the administration of ESEA. They were undertaken on a coordinated basis beginning with fiscal year 1969 and, under the bureau house rules, preempted all individual program reviews, such as Title I. Generally, the purposes of these reviews were to take a close look at the management needs and capabilities of the state educational agencies in all areas of administration and then to recommend organization, staffing, and managerial improvements to enhance their functioning. In effect, the state agencies were receiving the benefit of USOE management and program expertise to improve themselves.

Internal bureau efforts by the advocate staff of Title I to have these management reviews look critically at the state enforcement practices of Title I and other ESEA policies were consistently rejected by the bureau leadership, which had been assumed by Leon Lessinger, fresh from San Mateo, California, in 1968. As a result, the reviews overlooked Title I deficiencies in the state agencies on such vital subjects as review procedures for Title I projects to detect local district failures in achieving fiscal comparability, concentrating Title I funds, involving parents in the projects, limiting the project areas, and otherwise improving project quality through enforcement of USOE's basic criteria. As an example, the states of Florida and Tennessee were notoriously weak in their review and approval of local district applications, in the leadership of their districts, and in their enforcement of the basic criteria. As a result, the programs in those states were very ineffective—Florida's projects were loaded with "hardware," and Tennessee's were thinly disguised general aid to all schools. Yet the State Management Reviews of these states in 1969 barely mentioned the deficiencies and empathized with the states in their expression of need for staff and improved state policies on salary and personnel. The opportunity to carry out federal compliance monitoring never materialized through the management review device. Instead, this task fell directly on the shoulders of the limited Title I staff.

TITLE I INTERNAL MONITORING

Not only was the Title I staff of the Division of Compensatory Education too limited for the enforcement effort required, but such an effort was a challenge to a key part of the USOE code of behavior. That is, states have been expected—and assumed—to live up to their agreements, and USOE has traditionally been loath to assume that they would do otherwise. The problem was that ESEA Title I posed a new set of circumstances for this peaceful scene. In addition to being large and highly visible, it has a "national priority" in terms of its concern for the poor. And Title I rests on a new assumption in USOE federal-state relations: signed "assurances" that the state agencies will enforce the federal requirements—whatever they may be. These assurances *legally* commit the state to federally initiated enforcement actions.

At the outset of Title I, USOE planned to monitor state agency performance under the assurances with a field staff, for which 30 positions were requested, to be placed in the nine DHEW regional offices. Ten of these positions were initially allocated to Title I, and they lasted only a very short time before they were reassigned, via USOE reorganization, to general "elementary and secondary" duties during 1967. In 1968 all these field positions were completely eliminated by budget action forced by the Congress as a result of pressure being brought by the chief state school officers. Behind the pressure was a move by the chiefs to forestall decentralization of USOE activity, which they distrusted as a device for severing their Washington contacts. So field surveillance of Title I compliance by the states never got going in the critical early years. In the absence of a Division of Compensatory Education mandate or staff to monitor the states, almost complete reliance had to be placed on the integrity and the ability of the state agencies to comply with both the letter and the spirit of federal policy requirements. This compliance would occur only where a competent state Title I coordinator—usually supported by a strong improvement-minded chief—was on the job to make it happen. Unfortunately, most states did not produce this combination, and USOE had never learned to differentiate among the states on the quality of their performances. Mississippi was suddenly to reveal all of this—to a lot of people.

In the early spring of 1969, a series of complaints hit USOE from Mississippi outlining egregious abuses of Title I programs on a state-wide basis and in 12 districts in particular. This series was sparked by the NAACP Legal Defense and Educational Fund, and the documentation of these complaints was clear and specific. The Title I staff tactics shifted from routine referral of complaints to the state for investigation and report to an inquiry addressed to both the state and the local complainant. When the dual responses revealed a complete state cover-up of the local school boards combined with a clumsy contradictory explanation from the state chief on its practice for disclosing project documents to public inquiries, USOE took investigative action.

Despite traditionalist efforts in the Bureau of Elementary and Secondary Education to confine the Mississippi review to an inquiry into the state's "public information" practice, the Division of Compensatory Education was able to launch an across-the-board investigation of the Mississippi program during the summer of 1969. This investigation (discussed in greater detail in chapters 4 and 6) revealed to USOE authorities the dangerous game they had been engaged in for four years; namely, relying on paper assurances from state chiefs who had no intention of honoring their sworn commitments to administer Title I funds for the exclusive benefit of poor children in their respective states. In the face of incontrovertible evidence. Mississippi readily acknowledged in July 1969 its deficiencies in applying the federal Title I criteria and subsequently agreed to federal enforcement action to correct such abuses as the gross lack of comparability in the allocation of local funds. In turn, Mississippi's action placed on USOE a responsibility to determine its position on these matters with all states. USOE itself was now on the firing line because of its own laxity. With its typical monitoring activities being deemed insufficient, USOE created a special task force on Title I.

USOE TITLE I TASK FORCE

In response to the direct challenge to its position as posed by the Mississippi investigation and to the threat of continuing external surveillance, Commissioner Allen moved with unusual USOE vigor in the fall of 1969 to create a new climate of enforcement. A task force of 16 persons with a budget of $1 million was assembled in November 1969 with a mandate to review in depth eight major areas of Title I administration and to recommend action on such major problem areas as comparability of local expenditures, monitoring of state performance, organization of program activity, and relation of Title I to other DHEW programs. In the organization of this task force review, Allen took deliberate pains to bypass the traditionalist Bureau of Elementary and Secondary Education organization level to assure the treatment of Title I problems at a higher level of consideration.

As a major test of policy enforcement, the task force took on the issue of "comparability" of local expenditures and designed a set of reporting procedures that would force the state and local educational complex into compliance by producing data on a school-by-school basis. A new program guide was drafted, cleared with selected state agencies and various professional associations, and then issued by Allen on February 26, 1970. His timing could not have been worse. At that moment the House and Senate conferees on the ESEA amendments were arguing their respective versions of the changes in Title I. A strong Senate provision on comparability had already been informally agreed to by the conferees but Allen's issuance of the guide alerted and excited House conferees, sparked by Roman Pucinski of Chicago, who had no such provision in their bill, to object to this "premature" exercise of authority by USOE. A compromise provision on comparability was then negotiated by the conferees, and it postponed the effectiveness of the comparability requirement to fiscal year 1973 Nevertheless, comparability as a concept had now grown from an administrative tactic to a legal requirement, and the move was on to force the schools into compliance with the equal protection clause of the Fourteenth Amendment.

If belatedly, USOE was slowly turning in the direction of enforcing its own policies—a particularly difficult position to take in view of both historical precedent in education politics and its own general allegiance to the educational establishment. Title I, because of its funding size and its linkage to the poverty programs of the opportunity strategy through its enabling legislation and its subsequent guidelines, has proved—and still continues—to be a grueling test of USOE's capacity to exercise effective leadership at the national level.

From the standpoint of the federal level, the Title I experience has demonstrated numerous problems which must be effectively dealt with if a new national strategy for education is to accomplish the mission which Title I has begun. Among these problems are the construction of the legislative mandate itself; the federal role to be taken—both in terms of constitutional precedent and practical necessity; the development and use of advocacy; the administrative power and leadership of the agency to which the legislative mandate is assigned; the policy interpretation, structuring, and priorities given to such a mandate; the nature of the educational establishment itself at all levels and its general resistance to change; and the recipients of program benefits under such legislation. Moreover, the Title I experience at this level has also provided some clear evidence on the kinds of solutions that are needed for these problems, such as the need for clear policies right from the start, new kinds of administrators at various levels working cooperatively together, adequate administrative power to carry out program missions, broad-based and articulate advocacy, and techniques for gaining the necessary leverage to effect changes within school systems. At the other levels of the establishment, the stormy course through which Title I has traveled further illuminates these problems and the kinds of solution requirements that will be needed, as well as pointing up additional problems and potential solutions. With these considerations in mind, the Title I experience at the state level is next analyzed.

4

The State Scramble
Over Administrative Powers

THE SEVERAL LEGISLATIVE PIECES OF THE OPPORTUNITY STRATEGY in combination with shifting state and local power bases during the 1960's upset the existing administrative and political arrangements in education among the federal, state, and local levels—arrangements that had operated with comparative peace and tranquility in the past. In seeking to overcome the twin problems of economic dependency and discrimination, the Economic Opportunity Act and the Civil Rights Act were also seeking ways to bypass those social institutions and attitudes that tacitly or deliberately had contributed to these problems. Sooner or later the schools, as a highly visible social institution faithfully mirroring the prevailing attitudes of the local power structures which excluded the poor, were going to be directly challenged on their programs and practices as they related to the minority and poverty child. Indeed, the challenge was already apparent in the bypass of the educational establishment at all levels through such education programs as Head Start.

When the Elementary and Secondary Education Act emerged from the legislative process in 1965, reflecting the poverty thrust in the form of Title I and placing major new administrative demands upon the state educational agencies for its successful implementation, the stage was set for challenging not only the programs and practices within the schools for poor and minority children but also the time-honored concept of state leadership and control over education. Moreover, this challenge was coming at a time when financial resources were eroding for most local districts. In combination, they would produce a scramble over power at the state level involving jurisdiction as well as decision-making. The term "scramble" is used because there would be attempts to avoid assuming power, as well as attempts to acquire it. Most of the states were to discover that much of the new power assigned to them was highly distasteful, such as the enforcement of ESEA Title I requirements. In order to understand the ensuing scramble at this level, a brief look at the federal, state, and local educational relationships before the advent of the War on Poverty and ESEA is essential.

Previous Power Arrangements

Until ESEA, federal education acts had never challenged the authority and responsibility of the states for public education.[1] State legal control over public education coupled with unrestricted local authority over the operation of the schools have endured for over a century as the centerpiece of education's political mythology. Beginning with the Vocational Education Act of 1917 and continuing through the National Defense Education Act of 1958, the central concept was that limited categorical federal aid to elementary and secondary schools should proceed to the state and thence to the local agencies. One of this concept's corollaries was for the Congress in writing education laws to deal with all states as if they were exactly the same, regardless of their competencies. To differentiate between the relative educational strengths of New York and California as contrasted with the feebleness of Alabama and North Dakota was not politically very bright. A second corollary was for the Congress to assume that the educational establishment would deliver appropriately on whatever the missions of the legislation happened to be. Since such missions were usually worked out in conjunction with the establishment's perception of them and involved comparatively limited sums of money, few problems were encountered.

For two main reasons, the state and local educational relationships were also without challenge from the state level. One of these has been the manner in which state and local educational jurisdictions have divided up the turf. That is, in establishing state educational agencies and in defining the jurisdictions of local agencies, state legislatures have generally decreed that local authorities will run the affairs of the schools and that (except in the deep South) local funds will provide the major support for them. State supervision over school affairs has typically been limited to the certification of teachers and textbooks, the collection of reports, and the distribution of state and federal aid. Local educational authority has been reinforced by state-sanctioned local school boards, whose members govern the taxing of property for school support and, in turn, petition state legislators for continuation of their authority.

The other reason deals with the contending forces in the politics of virtually every state—rural areas, suburbs, and large home-rule cities—as they relate to the financial resources for education. In this struggle, the rural areas, which have always had power in the state legislatures, and the suburban areas, which have steadily gained power in the legislatures, have constituted a consistent, if unformalized, "alliance of the status quo" against the escalating demands of the financially hard-pressed cities for increased state support of education. At heart, this alliance between the rural and suburban areas has been an economic one, involving both the maintenance of control over local taxing power and the avoidance of an additional state-wide tax for educational financing, for which the cities have been pressuring. By the mid-1960's, large city school systems were approaching despair with regard to securing state solutions to their fiscal problems. Nevertheless, at the state level of educational governance, the net effect was a deceptive and fragile calm induced by the political stalemate over educational financing.

In contrast with the fiscal area, the calm of the educational establishment in the program area was genuine. That is, both the states and their local districts generally assumed that the kinds of educational services that were being offered to the students— middle class and poverty alike—were basically the right ones. In this latter area, the states let their local districts alone and the local districts were generally well-satisfied with the arrangement.

The net result of the arrangements in the fiscal, programmatic, and governance areas was a tranquil scene, in which the relatively small-scale categorical funds for the schools flowed serenely from federal to state to local levels with hardly a ripple of political concern. The states were willing to serve as middlemen in gaining whatever federal funds they could from the federal formulas, and the local districts were fully responsible for the performance of the schools in using the funds. For its part, USOE, under the ever-watchful eye of the Congress, was eager to avoid complaints of interference with local schools from state congressional delegations. As long as there was either a tacit agreement or an unacknowledged stalemate maintained at all levels by the politicians and the educational administrators that these conditions should prevail, this power arrangement, whereby the states held de jure— but not de facto—authority and responsibility for public education, could creak along.

Without the anti-poverty thrust that surfaced in ESEA through Title I with its target population, the power arrangement among the several levels of education, as well as the mythology of state control over education, might have gone unchallenged. For in passing ESEA, the Congress had responded to the potency of the mythology by returning to the traditional federal legislative pattern of federal to state to local authority. This pattern basically prevailed, even though some doubts about state-level capabilities could be read in the bypass of the state jurisdiction in two of the five original titles of the Act and in the state bypasses in the Economic Opportunity Act and the Civil Rights Act of the preceding year. However, the winning out generally of the political mythology also carried with it increased responsibility and authority for the states. Title V of ESEA provided money for the administrative strengthening of the state educational agencies. And Title I conferred broad authority on the state agencies either to approve or to disapprove local plans for expenditure of the federal funds, although the actual allocation of funds was made on a county-by-county basis and the states could not alter these allocations. Whether inadvertently or deliberately, ESEA—and more specifically, Title I—had set the first national test of state control over education. Assisting in this challenge was the impact of the other anti-poverty education programs of the opportunity strategy, like Head Start. Within five years, the myth of state control over education would lie in fragments, along with the tranquil façade of education politics.

As the generally traditionalist state agencies scrambled to gain power over programs and functions which appealed to them and to avoid power over those which did not, they would clearly reveal their problems with the local agencies in several key areas of administrative power. These areas can be defined as: (1) *enforcement*, the requirement of compliance with federal rules; (2) *control*, the de jure and de facto authority over local decision-making in key educational areas, such as the priorities for expending funds; and (3) *leadership*, the ability to determine valid priorities and to influence the local agencies to use them in the effective development and implementation of programs for children and youth. It has been around these three crucial areas that the struggles between the change advocates and the traditionalists have largely ensued at the state level. And firing the opening volley at the existing power arrangements were the hard-pressed big city school districts.

The States and Their Big Cities

Accustomed to going their own ways without any real interference from the state level, the agencies of the big cities (population of one million or more) posed major problems right from the start to their states in the aspects of control over local decision-making and enforcement of federal requirements—and subsequently to the Federal Government as well. These agencies were soon out to one-up the states on their knowledge of the amounts of money to be spent, the timing for receiving money, and the ground rules for its use. Since several of their superintendents, like Ben Willis of Chicago and Bernard Donovan of New York, had been prom-

inent in the legislative process of ESEA, they were not about to
take a back seat to their chief state school officers. Also, compli-
cating the state-local role was the fact that by 1965 all major city
school agencies had been caught in the fiscal vise of rising budgets and eroding revenues, and they were well aware that state
sources of revenue were closed to them. In combination, these
conditions led to the confrontations over local decision-making
and enforcement that upset the previous power arrangements. In
these confrontations, Chicago led the way.

CHICAGO

The launching of ESEA Title I was accompanied by an explo-
sive showdown between the U. S. Commissioner of Education,
Francis Keppel, and the Illinois Superintendent of Public Instruction, Ray Page, over the first-year Title I funds for Chicago. Illinois became eligible to receive federal funds on September 23,
1965, and Chicago was first in line to claim its new funds, amounting to $31.2 million, with only two massive and vaguely worded
projects. Chicago was already under a civil rights investigation,
growing out of a complaint filed by the local Coordinating Council of Community Organizations that the schools were discrimi-
nating against black students and teachers. Confident that the
discriminatory charges would soon be upheld, Mr. Keppel wished
to have at his disposal the maximum leverage possible to achieve
compliance with federal civil rights policy.

Therefore, as a means of averting new and major illegal use of
federal funds, Keppel, operating in the role of an advocate of
change, wrote to State Superintendent Page requesting that the
state approval of pending Title I applications from Chicago be
withheld by the state until the civil rights investigation was
nearer to completion. As authority for his request to Page to delay
the Chicago project approval, Commissioner Keppel was relying
on the provisions of Title VI of the Civil Rights Act for deferring
funds of districts found to be in non-compliance with federal desegregation guidelines. In choosing this authority, he gave both
Page and Chicago Superintendent Willis a basis for challenging

his action on the lack of documented federal evidence of de jure segregation in Chicago. Keppel, by his choice of the Title VI authority, abstained from testing the new withholding provisions of ESEA Title I itself, which would have to be based on a failure of the Chicago district to provide the state agency with adequate assurance of its intent to abide by the quality requirements of the Title I statute. These latter grounds actually would have been defensible in terms of the slipshod nature of the Chicago Title I projects; and by placing the burden of proof on the state of its propriety in approving the Chicago projects, the Commissioner would also have gained valuable time for carrying on the civil rights investigation.

In making this request to the state, a courtesy copy of Commissioner Keppel's request letter of September 30, 1965, was also simultaneously sent to Chicago Superintendent Willis. Without waiting for Superintendent Page to react, Willis immediately proceeded via Mayor Richard Daley to bring political pressure through the White House on Commissioner Keppel to release the federal funds to Chicago. Within five days, Willis was successful, and the state was relieved of the federal embargo. In return, as federal face-saving, promises were given by the Chicago schools to reaffirm earlier resolutions to end discrimination, including a restudy of its school district boundaries. Such face-saving did not, however, include Keppel; his days were numbered. Indeed, the Chicago experience of Commissioner Keppel is generally acknowledged by him to have hastened his departure from USOE in December, 1965, following a fit of LBJ temper.[2] Also, Page openly attacked Keppel for his interference in a "state" responsibility and made use of the incident in his next successful campaign for reelection.[3]

Again, in the spring of 1966, USOE, now under Keppel's successor, Harold Howe II, requested the state to delay the commitment of funds to Chicago and to investigate fully the now well-documented complaints of Title I illegality, such as the intensification of inappropriate services and the use of funds in ineligible schools. The state obliged by inviting the federal officials to confront the Chicago superintendent with these demands, and

also agreed to call such a meeting in its Chicago office. State officials were frank to admit that a direct showing of federal "clout"
would be required to gain any compliance from the Chicago superintendent. At a meeting thus arranged on April 5, 1966, in Chicago, federal representatives gave point-by-point criticisms of the
Chicago program to assembled state and local officials, including
Willis, and asked for revisions to meet federal specifications. At no
time during these negotiations did state officials offer to do more
than to relay federal instructions, to tape record the Chicago meeting, and to request procedural response by Chicago school representatives, who subsequently made only token changes in their
program.

Continued evidence that Chicago was flaunting federal requirements evoked from Commissioner Howe on May 11, 1966, a call for
a special fiscal audit of the Chicago program to determine the le-
gality of all of its Title I expenditures. When the audit findings
disclosed that the city had violated federal requirements by
spreading the Title I program to non-eligible schools, paying illegal overtime to teachers and to other staff, earning interest on
funds deposited in local banks, and ignoring all procedural and
deadline instructions, the state was quick to plead the case of the
local district before USOE. Specifically, it asked forgiveness for all
the Chicago misdeeds—except for the bank interest which they
agreed to repay—arguing the case of pressure to get the Title I
program underway during the hectic first year. Also, it was acknowledged by the state that changes would be possible under a
new Chicago School Superintendent, James Redmond, and that
he should be given his chance to reform Chicago without a multi-
million dollar Willis debt hanging over his head. At no point during the audit proceedings did the state acknowledge the local
violations—or the state acquiescence in them. Rather, the state
asked only that USOE waive the violation on the basis of the unusual first-year circumstances, which was still being negotiated in
1972.

The Chicago experience, involving all three levels of educational governance, was of major significance to the implementation of Title I. On the one hand, the experience demonstrated the

strength of the political forces that could be brought to bear on USOE. And it exerted a continuing negative influence on the power of USOE to exercise program controls—called for by ESEA—over politically active chief state school officers and city superintendents. USOE's position had been compromised as well. Indeed, the experience had forcibly demonstrated that being an advocate of change could have serious consequences. On the other hand, it demonstrated what was to become the typical pattern of weakness and avoidance of the states in the critical leadership areas of enforcement and control.

NEW YORK CITY

While the State of New York had taken a less deferential attitude toward New York City in comparison with that of Illinois toward Chicago, the school system of New York City nevertheless represented a formidable power and a hopeless administrative morass.[4] New York City preferred to be treated by USOE as a separate "state" and asked for the direct federal transmission of instructions to the city (to which the state acceded) since the New York City officials claimed that Albany was keeping them in the dark as to federal policies. One contributing factor to the independence of New York City school officials was the key congressional positions held by New Yorkers on the U. S. House and Senate legislative committees. City Superintendent Bernard Donovan was confident that at a critical moment the New York congressional delegation had sufficient clout to bring state and federal officials into agreement with city decisions. An additional factor present throughout the proceedings of the first-year operations was the assumption of city officials that the state office would finally endorse the city actions without serious challenge. Indeed, New York City, in the first year of Title I, was well along in spending its $65 million authorization before the state received any formal application from the city.

In fact, it was only through a federal inquiry about the city program in the early spring of 1966 that New York City's overly loose bookkeeping control of the federal funds was discovered. What the federal inquiry revealed was that instead of seizing the opportunity to take a completely new look at what they had been doing and then designing projects based on priority needs, the city school system had simply apportioned the Title I funds out to existing schools and activities on the assumption that the poverty-ridden schools of the city were already carrying out the Title I mandate. Administrative control of the New York City program had been placed in the hands of a budget officer who was busily engaged in maneuvering Title I funds from project to project in the "poverty" schools of the city. Requirements for specific projects and application forms had been summarily rejected as inappropriate for a city the size of New York, with the assertion that the USOE forms were designed for rural areas. New York City staff was "too busy" to gain the requisite data on which schools had the largest numbers of poor children and was using all-inclusive "poverty areas" of the city to distribute the funds. Also, the city school officials had arrived at an arbitrary split of its funds with the non-public schools (Catholic parochial and Hebrew day schools) which permitted these non-public schools to plan projects and expenditures up to an agreed amount of $15 million for their children. This split was arranged without any formal approval of the state. Subsequently, the state acknowledged that this split failed to meet federal requirements and could not be repeated. Buttressed by the federal inquiry and requirements, the state exacted promises for future compliance from the city, and the state also decided to assign personnel of its own to the city so as to be right on top of the action.

DETROIT

Another example of a large city school system that proceeded to expend Title I funds without regard to state enforcement and control was Detroit. That school system in the first year (FY 1966) of the program proceeded to commit its $12 million allotment to a variety of improper projects, such as:

1) Purchase of a Baptist church with $1.4 million of its funds ostensibly to house Title I activities, but auditors later found only a fraction of usage for this purpose.

2) Expenditures of $1.3 million in fiscal year 1966 and $2 million in fiscal year 1967 for "overhead" costs of the school system in defiance of federal regulations that allowed charging only new and additional costs.

3) Charges of $266,649 against Title I were made for ETV (Educational Television) services which were contracted with local funds prior to Title I.

With its purchase of the church building, Detroit wrote a new chapter in the book of ESEA church-state relations, since the auditors concluded that the only real beneficiary of the project was the Baptist Church. By its fattening of the Detroit "overhead" account, the system was assessing Title I with charges for clerks and janitors who were permanent fixtures on the Detroit payroll before Title I even arrived on the scene. ETV service charges were nothing more than a transfer of admission prices for Title I children who were already invited to the programs by the Detroit system using its own local funds.

In its zeal to expend the first-year funds, Detroit ignored warnings from both the state and USOE that the federal auditors would catch up with them. Having witnessed the federal retreat in Chicago in October 1965, Detroit was willing to take its chances with the fiscally timid "feds." And Detroit, like New York, was relying on friends in the Congress to bail them out of its difficulties if they arose. In disposing of $11.6 million of $12 million Title I funds available to it in the first year of the program, Detroit hit for an average of 96 per cent which was far in excess of any other major city. Friends in the Congress did seek to help Detroit avoid the penalty of its errors, as disclosed in an audit, through provisions placed in the ESEA Amendments of 1970 that would alleviate the Detroit audit findings related to "overhead."

These examples of big city one-upmanship of their state superiors would be variously repeated in Philadelphia, Boston, Los Angeles, and other major cities, as their superintendents set out to prove their ability to acquire and then to spend the new federal funds to suit their own local agendas. The result was that when the initial confrontations of the state agencies and USOE with the big cities had subsided, there were big cracks all over the tranquil façade of the existing power arrangements. Nevertheless, the cracks might have been repaired if the big city school systems had really known how to serve the needs of deprived children or the state agencies had been willing to utilize the opportunities of leadership afforded to them by ESEA in behalf of these children.

Such was not to be the case. In due course, the general inability—and unwillingness—of both the state and local levels to serve the needs of deprived children would demonstrate that the entire structure was in need of rebuilding. An examination of the typical patterns of state response to the ESEA leadership opportunities shows why at that particular level.

The States and Their Opportunities for Administrative Power

If the big city confrontations had revealed the weakness of the state agencies in terms of their de facto authority and responsibility for public education in 1965 and 1966, they had also given the states a legitimate and broad arena in which to forge a new administrative role for themselves. Both by Constitutional omission and historical precedent, the states and their agencies had de jure claim to this authority and responsibility. In addition, ESEA contained provisions which the states could immediately use to assert their general administrative authority over their local districts. In this manner, a major turning point had arrived for the states and with it an opportunity for them to change from being weak, traditionally conservative, rurally dominated dispensers of funds and collectors of information into genuine administrative agencies. ESEA provided this opportunity in all three aspects of administrative power—leadership, control, and enforcement.

The problem was that to capitalize on the opportunity afforded by ESEA through its various titles, the state agencies would not only have to change themselves, but they would also have to take some educationally—and sometimes politically—unpopular positions. Except for a few states, such as California, Ohio, and Connecticut, where the change advocates were able to influence policy, this opportunity for developing an effective new administrative role was frittered away in responses which showed little concern for, or understanding of, the substantive problems confronting public education. Among the many responses made, those which can be classified in the area of leadership, as we have defined it, have been perhaps the most revealing of the unrealized opportunity afforded by the five initial titles of ESEA.

When the individual titles of ESEA are interrelated in terms of the education problems they were directly mandated to solve, a basic strategy emerges. It was to mount a coordinated attack on these problems by initiating changes within the educational system by its professional establishment for the system's improvement. For this strategy to be effective, the state agencies had to be able to exert leadership with regard to establishing valid priorities and then to influencing their local districts to develop programs and procedures to implement them. That the states were crucial to the "improvement" strategy was revealed by the provisions concerning state exercise of authority within the various titles of ESEA. The combined effect of these provisions was a broad new mandate to the states which conferred more funds for and authority over education programs from federal sources than most agencies had ever received from state sources. For the most part, the states proved to be ineffective in carrying out their key role in the strategy. Illustrative of this ineffectiveness were their responses with regard to Title V administrative funds, Title III and innovation, and Title I's relationship to the Civil Rights Act, all of which are examined here.

Title V was designed to strengthen the state agencies for "leadership in education within their own states." And it is revealing to note the manner in which they perceived this charge. Not only did

they strengthen their own ongoing operations, but they also accelerated the rate at which they were "doing their own thing" of
internal administrative housekeeping. This fact was revealed in
the fourth report of the Title V National Advisory Council, which
could hardly disguise its dismay at the "general aid" approach of
the state agencies in the following enlightening statement:

> For general administrative purposes, the states had been
> using from 20 to 25 percent of their total resources (with little
> variation in a 4-year period). When they got Title V funds,
> they devoted 44 percent of their allotments the first year to
> strengthening themselves in that area.[5]

Additional indications of the ineffectiveness of the agencies with
regard to exerting leadership are revealed through two major recommendations in that report. One is concerned with the critical
need for the state educational agencies to begin "equipping themselves to cope with the critical urban educational problems," in
order to deal with "immediate crises" and to develop "long-range
strategies to forestall such crises in cities that have not encountered them."[6] The other recommendation deals with "the need for
more and better trained manpower for state departments of education."[7] An interesting feature with regard to these recommendations is that the charge was now given to USOE in 1969, rather
than to the states, to find ways to accomplish these tasks. The distinguished panel making these recommendations apparently felt
that the state agencies were either unable or unwilling to accomplish these tasks on their own.

Title III of ESEA affords another illustration of the missed opportunities of the state agencies to inject a serum of innovation into
the educational system. Of all the ESEA titles, III was the one
DHEW Secretary John Gardner was counting on to reform the system. Before his cabinet appointment in 1965, Gardner headed a
Johnson task force which, excepting Title I, blueprinted the ESEA
legislative proposal. Its report stressed the need for overhauling
school system operations and infusing new knowledge and practice
into its sluggish arteries.[8] A network of innovative centers, functioning on a regional basis under new local authorities, to bridge

the gap between university research and school practice was the solution which was translated into Title III.

In order to avoid the deadening effect of state control, the proposals were to come to USOE in Washington for approval with only the "recommendation" of the state required. Unfortunately, this one provision proved insufficient to stem the tide of mediocrity which flooded USOE in 1966 and 1967 in response to the call for Title III project proposals. With little concern for their relation to the target population mission of Title I and the "innovative" potential of serving poor children, hundreds of projects were "recommended" by the states and approved by USOE in a frenzy of activity to meet project deadlines during fiscal years 1966 and 1967. In general, these projects financed a smorgasbord of "educational centers" which merely embellished the extant educational symbolism of the schools, such as equipment and materials centers, without disturbing the schools' internal functioning. By the nature of the competition, the Title III projects went primarily to the wealthier and better-staffed school districts, and by local design they served the more able students of the schools. The placement of projects in such districts did not run counter to the program priorities of the state agencies, since very few of them had developed any new priorities which took into consideration the needs of impoverished children.

Disenchantment with the program first set in at the Federal Bureau of the Budget when the Bureau staff discovered that Title III was responding almost exclusively to the pent-up aspirations of professionals, rather than to the needs of children. Congressional dissatisfaction reached a breaking point in the 1967 ESEA amendments when Congresswoman Edith Green was able to restore state approval to the Title III projects, in the face of a revolt against "federal control" led by the conservative group within the Council of Chief State School Officers. However, what really interested the state chiefs was not the quality of the Title III projects but the acquisition of control over them. Also, aiding the cause of opposition to Title III was congressional reaction to an extravagant conference held in the summer of 1967 in Hawaii by USOE in cooperation with the Kettering Foundation. Congressman L. H.

Fountain of North Carolina found this affair much too flossy for his conservative tastes and called for an investigation by his Committee on Government Operations. When the committee report castigated the needless expense of holding a national education meeting of 1,000 persons in our beautiful—but much too distant—new state, the Title III star went into swift descent.[9] Belated USOE efforts in 1968 to invoke priorities in behalf of "disadvantaged" children as a result of such critical examinations proved fruitless since the federal commitments of 1966 and 1967 were decisive in controlling the available funds, which were already facing curtailment.

Thus, Title III provided yet another illustration of unrealized opportunities for leadership from the states, although in this instance, federal decisions played a hand in causing the demise. Squabbling between USOE and the state agencies over the decision-making authority for Title III obscured whatever possibility might have existed for the development of realistic priorities for the "innovations" which were intended. And the ESEA amendments of 1967 effectively terminated the hope that this phase of the ESEA strategy would succeed.

The third example with regard to leadership deals with the relationships between Title I of ESEA and Title VI of the Civil Rights Act. These relationships afforded a unique opportunity for the states—and particularly the southern states—to exert a leadership model of the highest order for their local agencies and the public at large in the sensitive area of school desegregation. While the focus in this illustration is placed on the performance of the southern states, it must be noted that the performance of many northern states was also less than adequate in this regard.

The southern states' response to this particular opportunity must be understood in the context of their evasion of the legal responsibility for implementing the 1954 Supreme Court decision (*Brown v. Board of Education*) as it related to public education. Only the border states of Kentucky and Maryland employed the authority of their state educational agencies to hasten compliance with the 1954 decision. Kentucky initiated persuasive action on its local districts in 1962–1963; and, in 1962, the Maryland Board of Educa-

tion reemphasized state policy to guarantee pupil assignments
without regard to race.[10] Otherwise, the state agencies took a
"hands off" attitude and allowed the federal courts to bring about
compliance with the law.

Even with the passage of the Civil Rights Act in 1964, the situation as far as public education was concerned still remained substantially unchanged. Title VI of the act contained, among other
provisions, a provision that any federal funds appropriated for
public education had to be used in a non-discriminatory manner
and, more specifically, a racially desegregated one. However, since
federal funds for education prior to 1965 were extremely limited
and were also earmarked for target groups that did not necessarily
overlap with those of the Civil Rights Act, many local districts
simply forfeited the federal money rather than face compliance
under Title VI. For their part, the state educational agencies,
mindful of political sensitivities, continued their "hands off" policy and let the Department of Health, Education, and Welfare
handle compliance with Title VI.

However, the passage of ESEA in 1965 created a new situation
for the southern state educational agencies and their local districts. This new situation was specifically created by three features
of ESEA Title I. First, the Title I formula was highly favorable to
the southern states in recognizing poor children coming from families of $2,000 annual income or less. With low wages and large
families, southern poverty was well represented in the formula
allocation of $1.2 billion. Southern and border states, having 33
per cent of the 1960 U. S. population (the census on which allocations were based), received 43 per cent of the first-year funds, and
by the third year the figure rose to 45 per cent. Second, the target
population of Title I—schools and children alike—was also basically the same target population on which the desegregation
process was focused. Third, there was the magnitude of the new
money, which was sufficient to bring a number of financially
starved districts into compliance. In this regard, Title I soon became a handy weapon for enforcing desegregation, either through
the courts or by means of administrative action.

Despite Title I's support through these features of Title VI of the Civil Rights Act, there was a danger in Title I that called for prompt federal attention. Specifically, it was a potential misuse of the funds to lock black children into the target (segregated) schools by the placement of all the Title I benefits in them. A conflict between the federal objectives of Title I and those of the Civil Rights Act was clearly possible, because of the use of school boundaries both as a target area definition and as a device for effecting segregation of children. An escape from this entrapment was achieved by Commissioner Howe in a policy announced on August 9, 1966, and reinforced on February 27, 1967,[11] which called for Title I services to "follow the child" from his segregated to his desegregated school and for the imaginative use of funds to attain the goals of integration.

The states were then asked to implement this policy by assuring that Title I projects, designed by local districts, employed this concept of the services following the child. Herein lay the crux of the leadership opportunity for the southern states. To little avail, the general reaction of these states was one of indifference and withdrawal from responsibility. Essentially, the local districts were placed on their own initiative to design "legally approvable" projects—which in some states meant the use of federal funds to reinforce segregation by placing Title I services, such as free lunches, in target schools (segregated), but not in non-target schools (desegregated). And the Federal Government was left with the enforcement of both Title I and Title VI requirements.

Georgia provides an example of a state that avoided the opportunity for leadership by continuing to "look the other way," as it had been doing since 1954. Some 30 Georgia school districts failed to submit acceptable plans of compliance with the Civil Rights Act Title VI requirements during the years following ESEA funding and thereby surrendered about $6 million in Title I funds to the compliant Georgia districts in 1967, 1968, and 1969. By its passive stance—or as one state man put it, "unwillingness to be a 'Civil Rights policeman' for the Federal Government"—the state permitted conditions of segregation to deny the children of those

districts the benefits of Title I. Also, the state was generally ineffective in the role of requiring compliant districts to make sound
use of Title I funds to see that essential services "followed the
child" from segregated to desegregated schools and of invoking
Title I as a positive force for desegregation. Federal intervention
had become a necessity. On December 17, 1969, Georgia became
the first state to be served a federal court order requiring state
supervision to achieve local school desegregation. The Georgia
ruling followed a Department of Justice suit against the entire
state, and both the lawsuit and the ruling were an innovation in
the legal arena. By the court order, Georgia was required to withhold state funds from districts which failed to meet minimum
standards set by the court, and the state was also told to monitor
local compliance. In focusing the legal action on state funds, the
court removed the onus from the Federal Government and placed
it on the state. Now Georgia was to become a policeman for integration, but a "State cop" rather than a "Federal cop."

It had taken 15 years for the courts and the Department of Justice to bring the states into the thick of the desegregation struggle,
using Georgia as the test case. By the same token, the southern
state educational agencies had successfully remained "in hiding"
from their educational leadership responsibility for that same period of time. They simply had been unwilling to take forceful action to lead their local districts toward the goal of desegregation
by the effective use of federal funds that would have greatly facilitated such action.

While the southern experience with a common problem affords
a glaring example of the necessity of bringing external force to
gain performance of their leadership responsibilities, the state
agencies in all regions of the country were generally lacking in
their capability for positive leadership in the critical areas of education priorities and policies. This experience further demonstrates
the failure of the basic ESEA strategy to initiate changes within
the educational system without sufficient leverage on its state establishment in the aspect of leadership. For the most part, the results would be much the same for the aspects of control and
enforcement as well.

If one major principle contained in the ESEA strategy was to strengthen the leadership role of the states, another principle was the sharing of authority and responsibility among the three levels of government with regard to the administration of Title I. This latter principle followed the traditional complexities of federal-state-local relations. In brief, the sharing principle was designed to work in the following way. Generally, USOE sets policies and allocates funds to counties. The state then allocates funds to individual school districts, interprets policies to them, and approves their projects. Local districts, in turn, determine the schools to be served, design the projects, and operate them following state approval. The states monitor the local projects, and the Federal Government conducts program reviews and fiscal audits of state agencies. Additionally, a set of assurances is given to the Federal Government by each state, signifying its willingness to participate in the program and stating its intent to administer the program in compliance with federal policies. Likewise, the local districts sign a set of assurances in their project applications to the state, signifying their acceptance of conditions and requirements set forth in federal and state policies.

Obviously, effective functioning of this administrative tangle calls for high degrees of trust, confidence, and capability among the three levels of government or, alternatively, for extensive policing efforts from the federal and state levels. If the key to the successful implementation of the shared responsibility and authority principle lies in the extent to which the state agencies take their signed assurances seriously with regard to program substance, the more typical pattern has been one of honoring the procedural niceties, such as compiling and filing annual reports with USOE, and fiscal mechanics, such as dispensing the money as rapidly and accurately as possible to their local districts. Indeed, both the haste with which all of the titles of ESEA were implemented and the early USOE stance on Title I, in particular, suggested that program substance was really not as important as the fiscal mechanics.

For example, some 39 states had already signed the required

federal assurances for Title I when the first congressional appropriation became available on September 23, 1965, and these states
were immediately eligible to participate. The remaining states
quickly followed. Since federal regulations had been issued early
in September 1965, all that the states needed to place their districts
in business were federal application forms and guidelines, which
followed soon thereafter. No state plans setting forth priorities to
be achieved in serving deprived children and strategies for achieving these priorities were required. In addition, the funds arrived
in the middle of the fiscal year 1965–66 for use by the close of the
year.

In the case of many school districts throughout the nation, the
entitlement resulted in very large sums of money—representing
major expansions of their meager school budgets—being placed in
the hands of thousands of rural superintendents and school boards.
These large additional funds made suddenly available for the
financially starved schools produced heavy pressure on both state
and local education officials to act without delay. Nowhere was
this situation more true than in the South, where school budgets
were increased by as much as 50 per cent. Immediately, southern
state education officials were faced with program and political decisions that made enforcement and control extremely difficult. To
explain, the special inequalities of black schools in the South were
well recognized, and these schools were obviously the prime target
schools for the new funds. However, excluding the predominantly
white schools from the new program would be politically difficult,
and one temptation was to find ways to "stretch" the target area
concept—a practice that would be present in practically every
state and district. Another temptation was to use the new funds
principally as an equalizer in the unequal school situation between
predominantly black and white schools. The third temptation was
to use the Title I funds to reinforce the existing pattern of segregation by concentrating all of the special services on the target
school campuses. Through this device, the disadvantaged minority
students would generally stay in schools where the maximum services were available, instead of taking a chance on the tokenly desegregated schools.

Mississippi affords an extreme example of what finally occurred as a result of yielding to the three "temptations."[12] While state policy generally identified the predominantly black schools for the location of the Title I program in recognition of the target area concept, the state followed this concept in ways that carried out its own agenda with regard to the several temptations. In this example, they are neatly intertwined.

In the local Mississippi Title I programs, a prominent feature was the location of new mobile classroom units—known as "Magnolias"—on the campuses of the predominantly black schools to house special and extra classes. One apparent reason for the purchase and location of these units was to offset pressure for placement of overcrowded black students in white classrooms—and thus avoid desegregation. Another reason was the simple fact that black school attendance shot up as a result of new free school lunches, a popular "equalizing" feature of Title I programs in the state. Also, the schools became crammed with equipment of all sorts. Much of this equipment was irrelevant, such as TV sets which went largely unused because of lack of ETV programming. Another popular feature was school band equipment and uniforms, although practically no children received such basic clothing necessities as shoes with which to walk to school. Programs were made available to the white schools by the device of locating materials centers and libraries on the black campus, but making their equipment and materials available "on request" to other schools. By virtue of better training, teachers in the white schools used this equipment and material far more than did teachers in the black schools.

If Mississippi afforded a striking example of state ineffectiveness, it was not an isolated case; other states—both North and South—yielded to the three "temptations." They were therefore defaulting on their assurances to the Federal Government and on their responsibilities to their educationally deprived children. The result was a clear demonstration that the principle of shared authority and responsibility among the three levels of the educational establishment as contained in ESEA was, with few exceptions, generally unworkable. In this regard, the outcome for this principle paralleled that of the leadership principle.

By and large, the ESEA experience has been one of neglected, and even avoided, opportunities by the state departments of education with regard to the key aspects of effective administrative power—enforcement, control, and leadership. What might have been hoped for as ESEA unfolded was that the state agencies would have seen and then capitalized on the opportunities afforded to them by this legislation. Indeed, a few states, such as California, Ohio, and Connecticut, did move to seize these opportunities afforded by ESEA and required that major changes take place within the state agencies themselves: changes which involved attitudes toward the purposes of education, the role of the school, the learning capacities and needs of poor children, and the re-ordering of priorities. In general, however, the states either have seen little need to change their styles of operation or, seeing the need, have been unwilling to take the necessary steps to effect their own internal reform. The few change advocates who did exist at the state level were usually completely outnumbered by the traditionalists, and thus the obstacles in their paths proved insurmountable.

From the administrative perspective, the particular experience with ESEA Title I has clearly pointed out that increased leverage on the educational establishment at the state level is needed, if it is ever to deliver on its avowed role of being the responsible administrative authority for public education. To achieve this leverage, stronger administrative and programmatic controls over the federal funds than those presently afforded by ESEA Title I are required. Such leverage requires new legislation which builds upon the hard-won experience with ESEA in general and Title I in particular. Indeed, what Title I has demonstrated as it evolved into the educational component of the opportunity strategy is that major reform is needed at the federal and state levels of the administrative structure of public education. The remaining level to be examined is the local one, and it, too, is in need of such reform.

5

Title I and
the Local Scene

TITLE I'S MANDATE FOR SPECIAL SERVICES and relevant education to
poor children caught the nation's local school systems with their
preparations down. Decades of experience with the complex problem of educating the children of poverty had produced a condition
of frustration and indifference in the local school systems, instead
of a stance of readiness for the task that now faced them. The
absence of carefully drawn plans coupled with the increasing federal pressure in 1965 to get going with Title I services, as well as
promises of increased amounts of money which never materialized, resulted in two general kinds of "instinctive" responses by
the local systems. One was to turn to the traditional services that
they had been providing to all children and intensify them. The
other was to meet the increasing needs of the school systems themselves, which presumably would also help to meet the needs of the
poverty children.

Whereas both of the local response tactics suffered from deficient planning, they were explicable in terms of the financial
pincers gripping the agencies. Urban school systems were under
particularly heavy pressure to serve their "high need" poverty
clientele, in the face of growing public resistance to increased
school taxation as well as to further student integration. Meanwhile, the unionized ranks of the teachers were pressing the

school boards and the superintendents for higher wages and smaller classes. In this predicament, it was natural for the schools to intensify, rather than replace, their existing programs. In the process of finding this tactic to be a loser, they would also discover that the middle-class value-system dominating their curriculum was a major hindrance to the success of the school's efforts. And it would soon become apparent that the changes that were needed ran much deeper than the vast majority of school people realized.

The resistance to change which Title I had encountered from traditional forces at the federal and state levels might have been at least ameliorated had the local systems stood ready—or even willing—to deliver on Title I's mandate to serve the educational needs of poor children. To the misfortune of the Title I children, the local school administrators were thoroughly conditioned to their standard programs which well served the middle-class child, but which usually shortchanged the poverty child in terms of program quality and resources. Equalizing the scales of local resources for the poverty child—and then tipping the scales in his favor with Title I aid—would prove too big a challenge for most administrators. But this challenge was precisely what Title I asked them to do, and the concept of genuine equality of educational opportunity was hanging in the balance.

That the challenge was recognized can be seen in the efforts of a minority of discerning people within the local-level establishment to effect the needed program changes in the system. These efforts were to create some hackle-raising conflicts that, in turn, have challenged the very existence of the school system and its insulated establishment. In some instances, these conflicts were to move a small number of local systems into evolving new ways of dealing with the problems of educating impoverished children. And in every instance, they clearly pointed up the several major program issues involved; specifically, resource concentration, compensatory services, and funding equality. The conflicts around these issues, as well as their varying outcomes, are focused upon here, including their significance to a new and more powerful national education strategy.

Resource Concentration—
Issues and Models

In its most basic form, the issue of resource concentration can be viewed as a logistical question: How many children should be served in how many schools and with how much money? As the Title I experience has demonstrated, the question has proved to be far more difficult to answer than the local school administrators initially realized. The answer called for more than the statistics on pupil participation; it involved philosophical, educational, and political considerations as well.

Philosophically, concentration directly challenged two assumptions that had long influenced the allocation of resources to schools within a particular local district. One is the division of resources in such ways so as to provide, theoretically at least, equal amounts for—and hence equal—services in each school. In practical terms, this division has resulted in less for the schools where the poor children are and more for the schools where the middle-class children are. The other assumption is the equating of the poverty child with the deficient child. That is, the schools have typically taken the view that the lowered educational performance of the poverty child is the result of (a) home failure, (b) child failure, or (c) a combination of both. By implication, concentration as a tactic of Title I rejects all assumptions, in that it proposes to increase the resource allocation for the poverty child on the theory that the effects of an inadequate environment can be overcome or at least ameliorated.

Educationally, concentration pointed up real limitations in the school program to deal with the Title I mandate. That is, within the legal target population, most school systems had about half of their schools technically eligible, based on the averaging of attendance from low-income families. However, if the schools were identifiable using the economic factor, the children themselves to be legally eligible had to be identified on factors of educational deprivation. The legislation did not define educational deprivation, and no effective screening device was available to the majority of the schools that would place the educational needs of children into a ranking in terms of importance to school learning. Such a device was needed in order to identify the particular children to be served within the school attendance area. With neither a legislative definition nor an effective screening device to go by, educational deprivation stood open to interpretation. Therein lay both the anomaly—or loophole—within the enabling legislation and a key limitation in the school program. In addition, school people consistently maintained the view of the school's role and the educative process as being basically limited to academic matters. The idea of the schools providing services that involved the most basic human needs—like health, nutrition, clothing, and rest—as a matter of educational needs was typically met by the rejoinder, "We are not a welfare agency." This stance was taken despite the fact that the effects on academic learning of inadequately met basic needs have been well documented.

Concentration also posed political problems. In calling for tipping the scales in favor of poverty children, the question became how far could this reverse favoritism go before the middle-class part of the community actively resisted. Since strong professional opinion held that if the compensatory effort was to be successful the costs of Title I services would range from 50 to 100 per cent more than the average costs for regular programs, reverse favoritism would be very visible indeed. When this problem was combined with the deepening financial crisis in those school systems that had the greatest numbers of poor children and with the federal funding policies for Title I that had the effect of providing less and not more money on a per capita basis each year, the reverse favoritism of concentration was inevitably politically unpopular. Rather than specifically identifying the legally eligible educationally deprived children and then limiting new services to them, the temptation was to serve all of the children in the target schools. But if the services mandated by Title I were to produce positive effects on learning, they would have to be carefully focused on the target group of children, rather than spread thinly across a major segment of the school population. Unfortunately for the children, most local districts succumbed to the political temptation.

USOE would also find itself caught up in the same temptation.

As the first- and second-year returns came in, it became clear that dilution, rather than concentration, had generally taken place. For example, in 1966 Title I services had been spread to 9 million children for a national average of $108 per capita rather than $213 for each of the 5½ million children counted by the formula. While the school systems were headed toward dilution, the USOE Title I staff was not. The new criteria issued in 1967 asked the school systems to increase the amount of the Title I funds spent to at least one-half of their state average expenditure per capita, which would mean about $300 per deprived child. Since the schools began the Title I program in anticipation of expansion, rather than contraction, of the federal funds for poor children, the schools would need to change the direction in which they had been heading during the first and second years. Accomplishing this directional change would be extremely difficult in view of USOE's past performance.

Nevertheless, Commissioner Howe encouraged the Title I staff who, by 1968, were working with a group of state representatives to develop a new and stronger guide dealing with the principles and techniques of program concentration. He endorsed the effort, while recognizing its retrenchment impact on diluted local programs, and then signed a strongly worded program guide that was all set to be issued in September 1968 to govern the local programs for fiscal year 1969. However, a newcomer to the USOE traditionalist forces in mid-1968, Associate Commissioner Leon Lessinger, became very worried about the political impact of a call for cutbacks in pupils to be served just prior to the November elections. He then persuaded Howe, who was preparing to depart USOE, to take two steps in opposition to the new strong criteria: (1) delay the issuance of any new policy guide until late November 1968 (after the elections) and (2) remove key words in the guide calling for strict dollar criteria for measuring Title I concentration. When the guide arrived in the field "a day late and a dollar short," the key state representatives who had worked on the original stronger version recognized with dismay another USOE retreat at a critical juncture in the contest for educational reform.

In spite of policy waffling by USOE traditionalists, some states and their local agencies took the concentration theory seriously, and their efforts are worthy of study. While all of the states gave official recognition to the new USOE policy guide on concentration, only a few of them—like Ohio, California, and Connecticut— were willing to take strong state positions in support of the policy. Following the federal-state lead, the larger local agencies in those states pursued policies of concentration and implemented programs for their most disadvantaged children. Three of them are examined here for their varied approaches. In each instance, the basic logistical question of how many schools and pupils to involve with the money available, as well as its attendant philosophical, educational, and political considerations, had to be addressed.

CLEVELAND

Cleveland's first round with ESEA Title I was marked by its prior entry into the war on poverty under OEO guidelines. Since these guidelines defined "poverty areas" within the city, these areas seemed the natural ones to use for the companion ESEA Title I programs. In a city-wide system of 151 elementary and 36 secondary schools, Cleveland found 71 elementary schools and 22 secondary schools in its poverty areas. Having thus located their first-year target schools, Cleveland proceeded to establish services for deprived children in these schools and soon devised 12 projects offering services which their "conventional educational wisdom" told them were needed by deprived children. Many of these services were hastily devised "extras," such as summer school, camping, field trips, and tutoring, which were easy to set in place while the system was groping for handles on their problem of treating human deprivation. By these means, Cleveland reached 55,000 children with $4.6 million in federal funds during this first year for an average of $85 for each participating child. Not much in the way of service to a school system already spending at least six times that amount on all of its children.

Although some adjustments were made in the second year, the real shifts in the program did not start until the third year when Cleveland came under the gun of the state agency in Columbus and the veteran Ray Horn, Director of Federal Assistance Programs, began to ask some tough questions about the vastness of the Cleveland program in relation to its meager results. By this time, USOE was now pressing the states for local "concentration" in the clear light of shrinking federal appropriations. Fortunately, Cleveland had also developed reliable data on the existence of welfare families by school attendance areas and was prepared to identify the "hard core" poverty schools on a ranked basis.

Based on these analyses and critical examinations of their practices, the school officials of Cleveland, led by their able Superintendent, Paul Briggs, and his assistant, James Tanner, decided that Title I funds in the third year were sufficient to serve only 20 elementary and 11 secondary schools. They decided that some 32,000 children were to receive the most successful services. In the fourth and fifth years, Cleveland found that shifts in welfare caseloads had realigned the highest 20 eligible schools. Therefore, they adjusted their program to include 12 new elementary schools (retaining all of the original 20 to avoid loss of continuity) and then cut the secondary programs to 9 eligible schools. By the fifth year of the program, they were down to 20,000 participating children, sharing in $6.8 million of federal funds. This reduction was accomplished by gradually weeding out projects that were not yielding results, and, by the fifth year, a target population had been identified that could be effectively served with the available resources.

At the same time, Cleveland was beginning to tilt its program in the direction of the youngest children, as against its previous program of thinly spread, across-the-board services for all deprived children at all age levels. What Cleveland found out and began to apply were three major principles. One was academic deficit prevention which, in Cleveland's case, has meant reaching the children before they have run into trouble with the key areas of reading and mathematics. The second was continuity of service to the same young children. The continuity principle has been difficult to apply in programs for the disadvantaged child because of his family's continual moving from place to place within the inner city. Typically, the schools in the poverty areas of any city have more than half of their children move to another attendance area within a school year. The third principle was having a common purpose or mission for all of its projects serving disadvantaged children. Specifically, it has meant the improvement of school performance by these children to the point that they function effectively at their appropriate grade levels.

The several principles have been combined in the following way. By focusing on their younger children and giving special attention to the skill areas of reading and mathematics, Cleveland has devised a ladder of program services that takes children at age four and brings essentially the same children through the primary years of schooling. This structure permits early screening, diagnosis of needs, prescription of treatments, and continuity of service to children until they are through the critical formative years of school learning. Also, it has included the element of early and continuous involvement of the parents and families of the children to gain the needed home reinforcement of the school program and to bring the strength of parent participation directly into the school program.

The results have supported Cleveland's use and application of the several concentration principles. Particular progress is to be noted in the Reading Improvement Project for children in grades one through three. In this case, the target elementary schools have been placing selected children in special daily reading classes for 45 minutes of intensive training from skilled reading teachers using special materials. By emphasizing small-group instruction (6-8 children), the program has been tailored to the needs of each child to give him the chance to proceed at his own rate. The service was costing an extra $221 per child per year in 1970.

A catch in this program has been that only half of the children who need the reading improvement in the target schools are receiving it, since funds have been insufficient to allow all of the children needing it to receive the enriched treatment. Rather than dilute the service to all, Cleveland has chosen to give it to a random selection of half of the needy children. Experimental and control groups were drawn between the poor children who received the service and those who did not. The results following four years of operation of this program have been dramatic. For each year of reading instruction, the children performed on the reading achievement tests, as follows:

1. Expected normal gain for average non-deprived grade level children—10 months.
2. Expected normal gain for deprived children prior to entering the Reading Project—5 months.
3. Actual gain for deprived children in the control group (no treatment)—5 months.
4. Actual gain for deprived children in the experimental group (receiving treatment)—8½ months.[1]

In summary, the reading treatments have restored a full 70 per cent of the reading achievement lag in these deprived children in relation to tested grade norms. When it is realized that these children were in the below-average group in reading scores, this gain is truly remarkable.

Another Cleveland effort has been successful in remedying the reading deficiencies of children who have reached the fourth grade. Beyond grade three, reading problems become more difficult to correct and call for more specialized services. Accordingly, those children, who by fourth grade are showing two grades (or more) reading retardation in the Cleveland target area, are carefully examined by a diagnostic reading clinic and are selected for participation in an intensive program of remediation. Pupils are selected following intelligence tests which rule out those not reading because of a learning problem (low I.Q.). Those accepted are typically found to have family, social, or psychological problems standing in the way of their learning, and these problems are attacked by a team of professional specialists in social work, psychology, and medical therapy who seek to ameliorate the external conditions which retard classroom progress for the children. Since the clinic is in a former school centrally located in the poverty area of Cleveland and serves all the target schools, the costs of transportation to and from the clinic are part of the project cost, as is the operation of the plant. These services are costing Cleveland an extra $800 per child per year. The results show that most children are returned to their regular classes restored to grade-level reading for their particular age levels. Since the children stay in the program for 38 weeks regardless of their progress, the maintenance of their gains is assured. Moreover, by seeing to it that the Reading Improvement Project is located in each target school, the attrition rate (pupils lost from the program during the year) is down to 12 per cent. In such evidence lies the principle of service so lucidly explained by the Cleveland experts—improvement in pupil behavior can be achieved if the prescribed treatments are delivered over a sustained period of time.[2]

In brief, then, the Cleveland Title I concentration model is characterized by the following features: centralized planning; the application of three major principles—deficit prevention, continuity of service, and an overriding single purpose of achieving grade-level academic performance in relation to age; and the beaming of the entire program at disadvantaged children from "hard core" poverty.

LOS ANGELES

Los Angeles developed a spread in its Title I program that was fully comparable to its well-advertised urban sprawl. Having found that about 180 of its 438 elementary school attendance areas met the technical definition of Title I eligibility, the city proceeded in 1966 and 1967 to give all of these schools a segment—however trivial—of Title I services. However, by 1968, it was becoming apparent that the Los Angeles system would have to make the decision to recast its program since funding of Title I was becoming increasingly restrictive. In Sacramento, the strong and forward-looking State Director of Compensatory Education Wilson Riles was applying mounting pressure to follow the federal guidelines. And the ineffectiveness of the thinly spread services was now obvious to all—the clients, the system staff, the state agency, and USOE alike. For example, despite Title I services for three years, the median reading level of the target schools had remained at the tenth percentile—when they should have been in the vicinity of the fiftieth percentile, based on standardized national testing norms.

Instrumental in the Los Angeles decision was a new Deputy Superintendent, Graham Sullivan, who arrived in September 1968. Having served as Deputy USOE Commissioner to Harold Howe II and well aware of the inadequacies of the Los Angeles Title I program, Sullivan began the monumental task of overhauling the city's ineffective program. In this task, he found a strong ally in Riles. The California State Guidelines of April 1969, which carried new policy criteria on concentration, were also in accord with Sullivan's views of Title I priorities. Aided in his task by the guidelines and the results of an intensive state program review headed by the capable Ruth Holloway, Sullivan placed the revised program into effect beginning in July 1969.

The revised program, using the State Guidelines, included the following key elements:

1. Concentrate the Title I services in the 55 elementary school areas that had the highest incidence of poverty—the inner-city area which included most of the black ghettos.

2. Insist on Title I supplemental services for all children to be based on $300 per child.

3. Place services in 15 junior high schools which serve the 55 elementary schools in order to maintain continuity of the services to elementary children beyond the sixth grade level.

4. Give priority to the following components which were to be included in comprehensive programs for all children who needed compensatory education: (a) language development; (b) mathematics; (c) parent involvement; (d) supplemental services; (e) in-service training of staff; and (f) overcoming racial isolation, including desegregation.

Accomplishing the redesign of the Title I program was politically and financially hazardous for the Los Angeles school leadership. Taking its $15.3 million of Title I assistance for fiscal year 1970, the administrators then added to it $9 million of related state compensatory education funds to be used in combination for the target schools. Since the additional sum for each child meant a 50 per cent increment in the $580 per capita local elementary budget, the schools involved would be receiving substantially more money and services than would the non-involved schools. Community disappointments at withdrawn programs were surmounted by a combined state-local position that held its ground. Intensifying the difficulty was the defeat at the polls of a proposed new school tax levy in the spring of 1970 which spelled deep trouble for all Los Angeles schools.

In redesigning its Title I program, the Los Angeles leadership has followed a pattern that has placed great reliance on the internal strength of the system to produce effective programs at the neighborhood school level. The pattern is described, as follows:

1. Working through the staff of the system, each school principal was requested to plan a program which provided for the effective use of the additional funds; and, when approved, to implement that program.

2. Local school advisory committees were established to work with each school principal and staff to decide upon, and then implement, the components of greatest need.

3. Longitudinal evaluation studies were set in motion to trace the progress of children and classes under the revised program.

A particularly vital function of the Los Angeles program has been the creation of local parent advisory committees. Having overcome the customary school system reluctance to admit parents to the Title I program, the Los Angeles system has gone the distance, after deciding that parents and advisory committees serve a useful role. On the average, the committees have included 15 persons, of whom at least half are parents with children in Title I programs. In addition, special parent advisory committees have been serving the Follow Through projects found in nine of the target area schools. One other feature of the Title I program revision has been the careful study of individual schools which had already achieved impressive and specific successes in compensatory education before the general revision. The intent here is to consider these programs as models for replication in other schools.

Illustrative of the Los Angeles concentration model is the 49th Street School in the heart of the black inner-city area. In this case, there has been a mixture of Follow Through, Title I, state, and local funds focused on an early childhood program which provides both instructional and non-instructional services. In addition to concentrating multiple services on the children beginning at age 4, these services have been provided on a continuous basis. Also, a major effort has been centered on involving the parents of these children in the educational program The school slogan, "Today's Readers Make Tomorrow's Leaders," was originated by the parents of the project children. The results have been exciting. Kindergarten-level children are reading and performing math at the regular first grade level. Parent enthusiasm has run through the school community, as these parents sense the means of escape for their children from the "failure-dropout-poverty syndrome" that has plagued their own lives.

In examining the developing Los Angeles model, several features are readily apparent. One of these is the program focus on children from "hard core" poverty, using a $300 override per capita per year. Another is to place the design and implementation of the program in each of the target schools and to involve the poverty parents in program decision-making—a potentially major step on the road to achieving local school accountability. A third feature is the examination of successful programs developed in individual schools as models for replication in other schools.[3] While the Los Angeles model has yet to be proved in the sense of a general upgrading of school performance levels, its design for decentralized planning around a set of six major priority components provides a useful contrast to the more centrally structured Cleveland model. One change is already apparent: A new spirit of cooperation has taken over the target area Los Angeles schools as the staff and the parents are challenged to plan creative programs at the school level, rather than having them handed down from above.

PHILADELPHIA

Like other major cities, Philadelphia began its Title I program in 1965 and 1966 with the intent to spread services to as many children as possible with the newly authorized funds. Also, like the other cities, it soon found that its funds were spread too thinly to have any real impact on the most disadvantaged children and that their achievement scores were showing no improvement from such scattered services. In particular, the school officials found that their program efforts at the secondary school level were ineffective.

Under the leadership of their youthful, driving Superintendent, Mark Shedd, the Philadelphia schools decided to try some new tactics. Since the city school system, beginning with the school year 1967–68, was living under the constant threat of a fund shortage and the forced closing of its schools ahead of schedule, the drastic retrenchments of Cleveland and Los Angeles were neither financially nor politically feasible. Instead, a compromise model was worked out which involved a retrenchment aimed at one critical age group in terms of school learning.

Shedd's tactics were based on the view, which he shared with other experts, that preventive approaches to compensatory education must begin early and that they must be sustained. This view suggested more emphasis on preschool and early childhood education. Accordingly, a plan was proposed by the Title I advocates to combine Head Start, Title I, and Follow Through in a broad attack on deprivation in the most disadvantage schools, focusing on children at age levels four through eight. Shedd agreed to redirect a substantial share of his Title I funds to augment a Follow Through grant from USOE that enabled him to place new programs for early childhood education in 32 school centers, principally in those schools where Head Start was already functioning. Through the combining of the three programs, a potential national model could be tested, which would involve a ladder of services for treating deprived children in poverty schools on a planned variation basis, and thereby could give a clearly directed thrust to Title I.

Through the use of a ratio of $4 of Title I funds to every $3 of Follow Through funds on top of the already operational Head Start programs, Philadelphia developed a much larger program than would otherwise have been possible. Moreover, Shedd convinced USOE that by experimenting with eight different Follow

Through program models, Philadelphia would provide a laboratory for the determination of the most effective types of curriculum for its inner-city population of poor black, Puerto Rican, and white children.

The plan in Philadelphia, as in Cleveland, has been to employ the principle of deficit prevention; that is, intervening in the learning process of very young children before the academic performance deficits become overwhelming. The principle of continuity of service for the age groups involved is reflected in the effort to use superior quality school programs as a stabilizing factor in the school population to avoid the pupil attrition rate so prevalent as a result of family mobility. Philadelphia—and other cities—has found that poor people will find a way to stay in the attendance area of a school that has a truly superior program for children. Most poor parents passionately want their children to succeed in school, knowing full well that this is their best chance for success in life.

Philadelphia's model building plan in early childhood education has potentially great significance. It serves as a major test of the view that the best strategy for overcoming educational deprivation among all deprived children lies in superior early intervention programs. It also serves to test a theory that major program changes at successive school levels can be effectively brought about as a result of making radical changes at the early childhood level, which, of course, means institutional change. While the Philadelphia officials are aware of this potential in their model, the growing financial crisis of the district precludes systematic planning for either expanding the early childhood programs or for beginning the overhaul of the upper elementary program as the next rung of the ladder in the model-building plan.[4] Thus, in its present form, the Philadelphia plan resembles a ploy rather than a major strategy for dealing with educational deprivation.

In summary, concentration models have helped to provide the answer to one basic question facing the schools; specifically, how many children are to be served in how many schools and with how much money? In answering this question, the school systems which took concentration seriously had to deal with philosophical, educational, and political questions as well. Among these questions were: How to redirect programs for increased educational payoffs when the finances and the politics of the local situation are unfavorable? On which educationally deprived group (e.g., hard-core poverty children with multiple needs) shall the main effort be focused, given the limited amount of funding available? What are the best age levels for dealing with deprivation in terms of recognizable and positive educational payoff? How much money on a per capita average will it take to secure this payoff? Inevitably, such questions, arising from the main one, led to the second major issue for the local districts—what services or programs are to be provided?

Compensatory Services

Like the resource concentration issue, the compensatory services one was also to prove very difficult. By implication, if not directly, Title I's mandate was asking for delivery on the local system's avowed purpose—to serve the needs of all of their clients. In mandating the schools to provide special services for their disadvantaged children, Title I posed a direct challenge to the educational establishments in the hundreds of local districts receiving funds. Specifically, their challenge was to assess the needs of the particular target groups of children and then to provide those instructional and non-instructional services that would assure their effective learning in school settings.

The local-level education establishment has proven surprisingly unprepared and unwilling to deal with the challenge. As has been noted, the view of the poor school performance of educationally deprived children as resulting largely from child failure, rather than from school failure, has produced a corresponding lack in systematic techniques by which to deal with the needs of these children in relation to school learning. Moreover, there have been the increasing financial problems of most local school systems. Also, despite the fact that most administrators have risen from the teaching ranks, they are not program trained. And even if they are, their administrative experience has conditioned them to view the "school" as the program unit rather than the child. That is, their budgets, plans, and personnel are developed in relation to specific school needs, such as the number of classrooms. This kind of thinking has tended to standardize the instructional and non-instructional services provided by local systems and inevitably has obscured the varied needs of different student groups. Then, too, the lack of planning grant requirements, the wide range of services permissible under Title I, and the pressure to get going have all contributed to the view that Title I really was thinly disguised general aid. Thus, the combination of these circumstances resulted in an approach emphasizing the repair of the system, rather than the design of new program treatments for a special group of children.

The systems repair approach typically consisted of intensifying existing services and stocking up on equipment and materials from the suppliers, from whom the administrators often sought advice. This approach would prove inadequate against the criterion of improved school performance by disadvantaged children. The process of finding this fact out brought revelations about school people's attitudes and resistance to change and some rethinking concerning the kinds of services that were really needed.

INTENSIFYING EXISTING SERVICES—
MORE OF THE SAME

Local administrators generally expected that the repairs of the system would occur at those points where the child needs were present. In short, repair the system and you are well on the way to repairing the child. Thus, in the more-of-the-same approach, the basic thrust was on adding to what was already there in terms of staff, materials, equipment, and facilities. Moreover, there would be an amazing uniformity and lack of imagination in this approach. Typically, it embraced more staff (such as teacher aides), more classroom services (such as remedial reading), and more special services (such as nutrition and health services).

In the case of nutrition and health services, the schools have fortunately headed in the right direction. It may be concluded that the food programs and, to a lesser extent, the health services have been the areas of Title I where intensification has had a payoff. While difficult to measure the effects of such education-related services in terms of improved academic performance—and, indeed, none of the evaluations of Title I have taken on this sticky task—there is little doubt but that such services increase the probabilities of youngsters being able to learn. For example, correcting a child's visual problem does not assure he will learn to read, but it improves his chances of doing so. By the same token, providing a malnourished child with adequate food which improves his attendance rate at school, not only increases his exposure to the instructional program but presumably gives him additional energy with which to learn as well.

With regard to the educational services, such as remedial reading, after-school programs, field trips, and the like, the more-of-the-same approach met with little success. The problem was that the same materials, attitudes, and people were all involved. It was still a case of fitting the child to the program, rather than one of fitting the program to the child. And the inappropriateness of that program—designed to fit the model of an average achieving middle-class child—for the child of poverty did not occur to the typical local school administrator. The local districts were slow to realize that major changes were required in the kinds of educational services being provided. Indeed, in seeking advice, local administrators turned more often to the suppliers of equipment and materials in the early years of Title I than they did to those who had genuine expertise in the educational needs of poverty children. And these suppliers had a lot to say—and to sell.

THE INFLUENCE OF THE EDUCATION INDUSTRY

Industry has provided the schools with more than the symbols of learning represented by textbooks, projectors, classroom furniture, and teaching materials. In a very real sense, the education industry has performed much of the "thinking" for the schools in terms of educational program. Through their research and development of the textbook market and its products, publishers have determined most of the textual materials available to teachers. By their design and production of classroom equipment, industry has set the teaching style of the teacher in the use of various media. Combining these ingredients, various companies, like Science Research Associates, have developed package curriculums which take much of the guesswork out of planning the instructional program of the school systems.

Thus, it was not surprising that industry was at least a step ahead of the schools in its alertness to ESEA and its implications for the expansion of their markets. A made-to-order market was provided by the ESEA Title II $100 million authorization for books and materials which were intended for all schools and children, including those in the non-public (mostly Roman Catholic parochial) schools. From this sizable toehold, the industry went on to provide much of the local "know-how" for Title I. Much of the industrial response to the mandate of Title I paralleled the school system response—of "fitting the child to the program." Moreover, this industry initiative caused school programs to emphasize the "things" of education rather than the "people" object of the program. Instead of taking a careful look at their own failures—the deprived children of their schools—the administrators turned first of all to the symbols of learning, the teacher's classroom equipment. And industry was out to sell the relevance of what they had, rather than to stop and consider the irrelevance to slum and isolated rural children of their white middle-class material and gadgetry geared to successful college-bound students.

As the first year unfolded, some zealous agents began to advertise "ESEA materials." One enterprising manufacturer of a planetarium managed to reproduce copies of an official state project approval of this device for a high school in the coal-mining fields of Pennsylvania, and then plugged it as a cure for educational deprivation. Also, the equipment displays at the mammoth annual February meeting of the school administrators in Atlantic City were devoted almost entirely in 1966 to "Title I ESEA equipment and materials."

Equipment and materials literally burgeoned in the schools as a result of the new Title I funds. Since most school systems were short on such items, their administrators collectively went on a buying binge without considering the relevance of the things they were purchasing to the special needs of impoverished children. In the area of textbooks and other instructional materials, they purchased more of everything, disregarding the fact that these materials were not being successfully used by the teachers of deprived children. When it came to equipment, two facts were conveniently overlooked. One was that teachers were simply untrained in the uses of many types of equipment, such as movie projectors; the other, that some equipment was inappropriate to their particular settings, such as television sets where there was no educational television programming. In some cases, expensive frills were added, such as the renovation of administrative offices complete with air conditioning, the purchase of expensive band instruments, and the construction of facilities with federal funds, instead of with state and local funds specifically allocated for this purpose.[5] Nowhere was the more-of-the-same approach better demonstrated than in the area of equipment and materials, and the children would soon demonstrate that this approach was no answer at all.

As it became apparent that the states were unable to apply the brakes to local "hardware" projects during the hectic first year, USOE set a cutoff date of May 2, 1966, on all local project submittals, and placed an embargo on all "capital outlay" projects—those calling for major construction or equipment purchases. By various kinds of restraints, the first-year binge on equipment and construction activity in the schools was limited to 31 per cent of the national total Title I expenditure.

However, not until challenged by strong-minded intellectuals, like June Shagaloff, Director of Education Programs of the NAACP, and by community action critics on the local scene, did the education industry begin to pay heed to the obsolescence of its wares. In addition, conferences held with industry representatives and curriculum experts at USOE began to elicit promises of new developments within the industry. Also, the 1966 National Conference on the Education of the Disadvantaged devoted major attention to materials which were relevant to poverty children.

Demands for "black history" and a "black curriculum" introduced a completely new element into the program needs of the school. And before too long, industry got the message that mixing a few colored faces in its textbook pictures would no longer satisfy the emerging protests of racial and ethnic minorities.

In sum, the systems repair approach to compensatory education revealed that it was no real solution to the problem of overcoming deprivation. Paralleling this failure of the school programs was the further revelation that the systems repair effort also had a fiscal side. Constituting the third issue at the local level, the belated efforts to achieve an equitable distribution of fiscal resources to the target schools in comparison with the non-target schools were to prove an even greater embarrassment to the local establishments than their largely unsuccessful compensatory programs. These efforts, which are examined next, challenged local fiscal integrity.

Equality of Educational Funding

In order for Title I to succeed, the new federal funds would have to be used only for the special purpose of helping poor children. This principle of special usage for new funds, in turn, assumes the equitable usage of existing funds, which has been termed "comparability" in compensatory education. Local school budgets are well known for their uniformity and their avowed distribution of funds on "averages" that presumably distribute the resources of the system evenly over the total student body. An assumption of Title I and its compensatory logic, is that the poor will get an extra share of the resources, after the even distribution has occurred. What needs to be examined first is the evenness of the existing distribution of local funds. On this score, local administrators often played games with Title I to make up for the unevenness in their local funds. A technical term for these games is "supplanting," and it is in direct opposition to comparability. Supplanting arrived in the early days of Title I, and the forms it took were varied, as the following incidents illustrate.

KINDERGARTENS IN MISSOURI

A common need of school programs across the country has been for more preschool services. In 1965, when Title I started, only about one-half of the nation's children of age 5 were enrolled in free public kindergarten programs. A typical midwestern reaction to Title I was to install kindergartens, first in the target Title I schools for all target area children and then later in the other non-target schools. Also, Head Start was adding to the momentum of this movement with its preschool programs for poor children. However, once preschool (or kindergarten) became available in a community for poor children only, the pressure became strong for the same treatment to all children. Reverse discrimination was having an immediate effect on middle-class citizens!

Local pressure was also exerted to continue Title I funds for preschool programs for the poor children, when these programs were extended to middle-class school children. When this issue arose in Springfield, Missouri, early in 1966, the local superintendent became embroiled in a community budget crisis that called for some midwestern fiscal prudence. In keeping with local sentiment for outside help, the Springfield superintendent persuaded the Missouri Commissioner of Education to seek a reversal of a federal policy that withdrew Title I funds from any new program when it became a general service for all schools in a district. The federal purpose was to avoid the use of Title I funds for the poor whenever local funds were used to serve the middle class for comparable services. A telephone call to Associate Commissioner Wayne O. Reed, the highly placed spokesman for the state chiefs within USOE, produced a qualified "yes" to the Missouri Commissioner's question as to whether or not Title I could be used as an "incentive" in this manner. If this answer had prevailed as policy, Title I would have been immediately reduced to a general aid-matching program. Fortunately, Harold Howe II had just arrived on board as USOE Commissioner, and when this issue was brought to him, he overruled his Associate Commissioner. As a result of Commissioner Howe's action, this potentially massive loophole in Title I spending was closed.

SUPPLANTING IN MISSISSIPPI

By far the most troublesome area for the application of comparability was in the South, where the remnants of the dual school system were still pursuing "equality" between the black and the white schools to lessen the pressure for desegregation. When Title I funds came into the picture, earmarked for the underfinanced and predominantly black schools, the temptation to use these funds to supplant local funds for equalization purposes was very strong, indeed. Because of its inability to enforce its policies by on-the-spot monitoring, USOE depended primarily on its fiscal audits to reveal abuses of the comparability policy—admittedly on an after-the-fact basis.

Although the DHEW audit reports in 1968 began to reveal comparability abuses in several places, an even more potent force for revealing such abuses soon came forward. The Legal Defense and Educational Fund of the NAACP had put its meager legal staff on the trail of abuses in the southern states; and, before long, some very expert legal talent became deeply involved in the integrity of Title I expenditures in South Carolina and Georgia, but with Mississippi as the prime target. In bringing a series of segregation complaints before the United States District Court, the Legal Defense and Educational Fund attorneys had also adduced testimony from witnesses which documented Title I expenditure violations as well.

Coahoma County provided a clear test case of Title I violations. Located in the Northern Mississippi delta region, Coahoma County, like most of its rural counterparts in the state, was systematically using the Title I program to perpetuate and to conceal its gross discrimination against black children with its own state and local funds. In order to safeguard its local funds in the event of a federal funds cutoff for non-compliance with desegregation, Coahoma County used Title I funds exclusively to pay for 35 teachers, 27 aides, and three janitors serving Title I project schools.[6] As a threat to the local blacks (and to the federal compliances forces), the loss of employment was used to forestall desegregation complaints. When the DHEW cutoff finally came on

February 10, 1969, in spite of the threatened layoffs, Coahoma
fired their Title I staff and closed the Title I projects. Since this
arbitrary firing terminated the contracts of teachers who had previously been employed with local funds, suit was brought in the
U. S. District Court for Northern Mississippi to effect their rein-
statement, supported by the Mississippi Teachers Association.
Other complaints were added to the suit, charging discriminatory
use of state and local funds in the services to black children in
violation of Title I's regulations and policies.[7] While the court test
of the Title I violations was delayed, the fact of their occurrence
led to an administrative remedy.

On June 23, 1969, U. S. Commissioner James E. Allen, Jr., or-
dered an investigation of the Mississippi Title I program. This
investigation by the Title I advocates soon revealed a consistent
pattern of wide disparity in state and local fund usage in 18 counties, including Coahoma. Unlike other states, the Mississippi state
agency had detailed information on the local expenditures in their
black and white schools as a result of reporting procedures, installed before ESEA, when the state was embarking on its own
equalization program. When target (black) schools were compared
with non-target (white) schools in these communities, the contrasts
revealed gross discriminations in per pupil expenditures and in
the size of local classes. On a state-wide basis, the USOE analysis
showed that 92.4 per cent of the black schools had expenditures
from local funds which fell below $200 per pupil, whereas 63.2 per
cent of the white schools had per pupil expenditures in excess of
$200. The delta town of Anguilla, located in Sharkey County, had
only two elementary schools operating, and the white school had
an average expenditure of $366 per pupil while the black school
was receiving $86 per pupil.[8]

In 12 districts visited by USOE investigators, the expenditure in
white schools was found to be 76 per cent greater than in black
schools; and the lowest average expenditure for white schools
($209.64) was found to be 12 per cent more than the highest ex-
penditure ($187.80) for the black schools in the 12 districts. When
class sizes were compared in these 12 places, it was found that
black schools had 30 per cent more pupils per teacher and 36 per

cent more pupils per class, than did the white schools. These discrepancies were not disputed by the state in its response to the USOE report of the investigation.[9]

Inequalities in the schools of the rural South have been cited with overwhelming frequency by the courts in their decrees outlawing segregation. Less well documented and more difficult to prove has been the inequality that exists in urban centers, North and South, where the differences between schools are often obscured by the sophisticated budget tactics of the city districts. However, these differences are also a target of Title I and its comparability criterion. The contest between Title I and traditional school fiscal practices has challenged the large city systems on grounds that were not anticipated by the draftsmen of the ESEA.

SUPPLANTING IN THE CITIES

City school systems have traditionally used their budgets and accounting systems to support the dual contention that (1) resources are being evenly and honestly distributed to all schools on an equal basis and (2) it is not feasible to provide precise and accurate accounting on an individual school plant basis.

Peering into this contention in 1964 was Judge Skelly Wright, who had been assigned to sit on the historic *Hobson v. Hanson* case in the District of Columbia. In a searching decree that carefully analyzed the pupil assignment and school administration practices of the District, Judge Wright found the Hobson complaint to be fully supported by the facts. In citing differences in the median expenditures of the elementary schools of the District for the school year 1963–64, the court found that the disparities identified the predominantly black and white schools. When arrayed by racial composition, the groups of schools ranged from $292 to $392 in median expenditure per pupil. In his June 1967 decree following this first lawsuit, Judge Wright dealt directly with issues of pupil assignment and segregation, but only generally enjoined the District school board from permanently engaging in discrimination based on economic status—he did not specify the remedy.

In mid-1970, the challenge of unequal resources allocation was reopened in a second lawsuit filed by Julius Hobson, with the assistance of the American Civil Liberties Union, against the District Board of Education. This time, Judge Wright, finding that conditions had remained unchanged in the five-year interval between the two Hobson lawsuits, decreed a specific remedy of equalized per capita expenditures for all elementary schools within a 5 per cent tolerance. Significantly, the District board accepted this judgment without appeal.[10]

In citing this example, it is to be stressed that the fiscal practices of the Washington school system are by no means an isolated case of inequality. The District of Columbia case is significant because of the precedent it sets for fiscal reform in the large cities. And it is to this issue of inequitable distribution of urban school funds that Title I's comparability criteria are addressed on a national scale. The magnitude of the challenge for fiscal equity can be seen in the delay in the impact of Commissioner Allen's comparability guide of February 26, 1970 (chapter IV). This delay was a direct result of Representative Roman Pucinski's objection to USOE plans to equalize the distribution of funds and teachers on a quantitative basis. Comparability as a concept poses a threat to the big city tendency to assign their least qualified and poorest paid teachers to the inner-city, predominantly black or Spanish-speaking schools.

Nevertheless, the particular test of the federal comparability criteria will crunch to a decision in September 1972, when all of the local school districts must prove comparability of local funds or forfeit their claim on Title I ESEA. When—and if—the contest is won, a major barrier will have been knocked down on the road to achieving equality of opportunity for all students in our schools, rather than just for some. The fact that the contest will occur at all is only one significant outcome from the struggles over Title I at the local level as it related to the issue of comparability. For this issue and the resource concentration and compensatory services issues, there are other such outcomes as well.

In general, the Title I experience has revealed that the nation's schools were in deeper trouble than even they had realized. The obvious needs of funds, personnel, and plant were visible to all in 1965. What Title I brought out of the shadows was that when the schools were challenged to educate the poor, they had little to offer. The demand for compensatory services for the poverty child produced an intensification of existing services predicated on the middle-class child. And in most aspects of the school program, such intensification did not result in improvements in achievement. A painful first revelation was the discovery that the schools did not really know how to go about the business of educating the poor. A second revelation, following hard on the heels of the first, was the realization that the deficient child concept was no longer going to be swallowed by the constituency to whom it had been applied for so many years. This constituency was now voicing a clear demand: "Teach me in a way that I can learn." In turn, there was a third revelation; specifically, the schools had no real plan or general strategy for meeting the child needs that now were facing them.

The signs pointing the way to the needed program changes were there—indeed, such signs had always been there. But like other institutions that have lost their way, the schools were not among the first to read them. In essence, the signs were telling the schools to treat their clients according to individual needs, to expand the concept of the school's role, to look carefully at the target population before designing the program, and to recast the neighborhood school as a center of learning. What all of the signs added up to was, of course, a need for broad educational reform in the program area.

Paralleling the program-area outcomes in significance have been those with regard to the public school finance system. In addition to the system's well-known inadequacy in terms of sheer amounts of money for education, local manipulations of Title I to lessen resource inequalities between poor and affluent schools have focused national attention on the fiscal inequities not only among the schools within a particular district but also among the local districts within a state. The burden of achieving fiscal equity has now been placed upon the school system. Although legally enforceable administrative policies emanating from the federal level have been delayed, court decisions in 1971–72 have put the large cities and the states on notice that the existing inequitable structure of public school finance at both levels must be replaced.[11] The question of whether or not this structure should be changed has ceased to be substantive; the question has now become one of timing and strategy. As with the program area, the struggles over the funding mission of Title I have underscored the need for sweeping educational reform in the fiscal area as well. Thus, the Title I experience has clearly pointed out both the magnitude and the kinds of reform that must take place in the program and fiscal areas.

In still another area, Title I, as the educational component of the opportunity strategy, has pointed out the need for major educational reform. This third area is the one of educational decision-making or governance. In a very real sense, the outcomes related to the governance area have largely resulted from the role played by the Title I clients—and more precisely, their parents—in their own rescue operation from poverty through the educative process. This role is the key to the planning of any future education strategy.

6

Education Discovers
Its Poverty Clients

DURING THE 1965–1971 PERIOD, the public schools have been re-discovering the public nature of their business. Simply stated, this business is to educate all of their clients to become self-respecting, self-sufficient, and constructive participants in society. The rediscovery process has been a painful one for the schools, since it has been initiated and sustained largely from outside the professional educational ranks, has clearly revealed the shortcomings of the schools and their current programs to the public at large, and has forced the schools into examining and then responding to the charge of having become self-serving institutions for their professional cadres instead of service institutions for their clients. Behind this rediscovery process by the schools and dedicated to achieving broad social reform within them has been the client advocacy movement. The main thrust of this movement can be described as the drive to gain participation in and control over the delivery of services to a particular client group—in this instance, the heretofore powerless and silent minority of the indigenous poor.

The concept of advocacy, which has given so much impetus to this movement, was initiated by the Federal Government through its programs under the Civil Rights Act, the Economic Opportunity Act, and Title I of the Elementary and Secondary Education Act. In essence, the advocacy concept, as reflected in these laws, seeks to place at the disposal of the client groups representing the poor the vehicles both for transit out of poverty on a permanent basis through such means as education and training and for gaining immediate leverage on their environment as exemplified by legal assistance in civil rights matters. In translating the concept, two general types of advocates have emerged—the poor in their own behalf and the professional on behalf of the poor.

While the client advocacy movement unleashed by the opportunity strategy has moved forward on a number of fronts, such as housing, employment, health and nutrition, its prime target has been the public schools—for various reasons. First, all children are potential, if not actual, clients of school systems, whereas with other agencies their clients must voluntarily declare themselves. In this sense, the public schools constitute a monopoly for the vast majority of clients; there is no place else for them to go. Second, the schools demand the presence of their clients for longer periods of time per day per year than any other social agency. Third, the neighborhood-oriented public schools as an agency are extremely visible entities; no other agency is so convenient to reach when it comes to protesting. Fourth, education is the well-publicized pathway to an improved standard of living. Finally, the school programs have never been specifically tailored to their poor clients' educational needs except in rare instances, and, thus, these clients have much higher levels of alienation from the schools.

Through the client advocacy movement, people who had been locked in poverty for generations were finally to demand that it was the duty of the schools to educate their children. This demand made it clear that they were now completely wise to the middle-class usage of the schools for upward social and economic mobility and that they were after the same usage for themselves. Activist groups among the poor began to register their bitterness at being victimized by school failures, and they began challenging the schools in two critical areas. One was the relevance of the middle-class program to poor and minority children; the other, the decision-making process within the system itself. While the poor did not invoke the well-tested middle-class techniques of elective school boards and active PTA groups for controlling school programs to serve their needs, they, nevertheless, would gradually emerge with somewhat parallel techniques for gaining participation in and control over the educational programs being offered to their children. In surveying the struggle for educational reform generated by the advocacy movement for the poor in the schools, there is the realization that the original view of doing something *for* the poor has changed to doing something better *with* and *by* the poor. And, through it all, the poor have found an effective—although sometimes ambivalent, contradictory, and downright confused—ally in the Federal Government.

If a valid plan for a new national strategy for education is to be developed, the efforts which the clients themselves have exerted must be understood and used as a foundation. Hence, this chapter is concerned with analyzing the parent-client advocacy movement as it moved from the phase of low-level participation in school programs to the phase of well-articulated demands for governance of the schools themselves. As a part of this analysis, the extent to which the institution itself has begun to function in the role of advocate in behalf of the clients as a tactic in educational reform is also considered.

Parent Advocacy

The client advocacy movement for the improved education of poor children began, innocently enough, with the parents of these children. Through the federal legislation, two types of involvement in education became immediately available to the poverty parents. One was through participation in the ongoing and new programs in the schools as aides. The other was through participation in the new advisory committees to the administrators and staff of educational or education-related programs, as typified by Head Start. For the aides, the path to involvement would be comparatively easy; for the advisory committees, it would often be an altogether different matter. As the two types of involvement began to unfold, the schools slowly awakened to the fact that changes in their usual modus operandi would be necessary.

TEACHER AIDES

An early impetus for the involvement of parents in new educational programs came from Head Start and its first summer program of 1965. As a part of the early guidelines for Head Start, OEO established a model requiring a "teacher aide" to serve along with a regular classroom teacher for each 15 children in a project. Aides were to be recruited from the poor without regard to academic qualifications. And parents were preferred. "Auxiliaries and volunteers" were also encouraged to assist the project and were, for the most part, to be recruited from parents and other siblings of the project children.

Title I of ESEA followed the Head Start lead in the employment of parents. With its more massive and continuous funding, Title I soon became the principal federally sponsored source of this activity. Once they overcame their professional "hang-ups" over qualifications, the schools took to this new form of employment with enthusiasm. Not only did they uncover a source of useful, low-cost staff for school operation, but they soon discovered that the aides and their volunteer helpers afforded a valuable link to the poverty community. In this latter role, the aides and volunteers found ways to improve the teachers' understanding of the children and to convey school objectives to the community for home reinforcement of the educational program. By the third year of the Title I program, there were 64,000 aides employed in local projects and 180,000 volunteers (mostly parents) who were serving the target population children in regular session and summer projects.[1] Thus, a new army of workers became available to plead the cause of education for poor children within the walls of the school and to interpret this cause to the community.

As the advance force for major change within the school, the aides have exerted a positive influence in the direction of changing teacher and school attitudes toward poor children and their families. Negative attitudes toward the poor are cited by most authorities in the field as the most pervasive influence against school success for poor children.[2] Both by their presence in the classrooms and by the force of their determination to help the children learn, the aides have helped to convince teachers and other staff that poor children and their parents possess the qualities of aspiration and motivation so critical to the school learning process. Of equal importance, the aides have demonstrated that these qualities, when appropriately tapped and nurtured by the school, will do much to reverse the effects of instructional programs which have been—and still often are—typically stacked against the poor.

On the employment side of the ledger, the aides are also breaking ground into the professional ranks as career ladders are being erected (again, under federal auspices) to bring these people into the professional world. Through federal programs, like the Career Opportunities Program and the Teacher Corps, the experience of the aides is supplemented by additional training in preparation for assuming classroom teaching duties. Also, many teen-age youngsters see these programs as an avenue into the teaching profession, as well as an "up and out" escape route from poverty. Moreover, varied innovative uses of aides have been devised by the schools, such as the use of high school dropouts for the double-edged effect that a learning experience has on both aide and child, and the hiring of male college athletes from the target group for their model-building influence with young boys. As a result of these new personnel arrangements, aides have provided a convenient meeting ground for the school and the community by serving the needs of both well. Schools have a newfound source of help to carry out their educational mission, and communities have found a way to penetrate the school environment in a constructive and acceptable manner. Thus, the two worlds of the poverty community and the middle class-oriented school have found a bridge to one another.

PARENTS AS MEMBERS OF ADVISORY COMMITTEES

While the path of aides to employment in the schools may have been smooth, the same cannot be said of parents who were seeking an "advisory" role in school affairs. Both Head Start and, later, ESEA Title I called for formal advisory committees to be composed in part (at least one-half) of parents of the poor children. Behind this provision of the federal guidelines was the creative idea of bringing the information and insights of parents directly to bear on the policy of the schools in the expenditure of federal funds.

Head Start guidelines gave a prominent role to local advisory committees. As a part of this thrust for community action, OEO was eager to create vigorous advisory committees dominated by their parent members, and the Head Start guidelines were both specific and strong on this point. Policy advisory committees (or councils) were required at the "agency" level, and committees at each Head Start "center" level were to be preponderantly of parents. Committees were to participate fully in the development of operating policies and to have a strong voice in the selection of staff for the projects. Professionals on the committees were warned against dominating the committee meetings, and parents were to be given decision-making experiences and listened to with understanding.

While Head Start projects gained rapid and widespread popularity as effective and innovative programs for young children, the administrative requirements raised the hackles of school administrators who were the principal grantees for the summer programs. Sharing power with parents over school appointments and taking advice from poor parents on "professional" matters were not in the book of the typical school administrator or his staff. Resistance to the advisory committees led to some withdrawals from the Head Start program, and the ripples that ran through the school establishment spelled trouble for ESEA efforts in following the Head Start model.

Title I advisory committee guidelines picked up the lead of Head Start, but did not go as far in their enforcement. In view of limited federal authority over local policy, USOE's program guides to the field took a much "softer" line on parent participation than did Head Start. However, USOE's growing conviction that strong parent committees were needed in Title I projects led to the issuance of a program guide in July 1968, using the Head Start model on local committee composition and functions. Since the Title I guide called for "new" committees to serve the projects, resistance from conservative states could be anticipated, and it came from the Midwest. Congressman Al Quie of Minnesota strongly objected to the required creation of "new" groups in the sparsely settled areas of his state. State objections were based on a desire to retain existing PTA-type committees, which were under the safe influence of the local Minnesota schools. Commissioner Howe, sensitive to the intervention of a powerful House committee member, acceded to Quie's insistence for this modification in the guide covering rural areas, where "existing committees" could meet the test of parent composition.

Despite its dilution, the new guide became an additional force for active parent participation since compliance by state and local officials has been slow, reluctant, and piecemeal. As a result of this foot-dragging, advocate groups locally began to cite the USOE guide as an enforceable requirement with local school officials. Thus, the federal requirement has served the cause of advocacy in two ways: by mandating effective participation by parents in ESEA Title I programs and by providing a ready source for complaints by local advocate groups in the event that the mandate is ignored.

ADVISORY COMMITTEES AND SHIFTS IN FEDERAL POLICY

From the inception of ESEA, the Congress was alert to the potential of parent participation in education programs. Initially, however, congressional endorsement for the concept of parent participation came in its committee reports and published committee hearings, rather than in statutory language. Taking what little encouragement that came from the committee reports and hearings, USOE moved rather hesitantly to advance the cause of parent participation. USOE traditionalist forces have resisted strong Title I guidelines in this area, as well as any amendments to accomplish parent participation through the legislative process. Nevertheless, before he departed USOE in December 1968, Harold Howe II sold the Bureau of the Budget on an amendment mandating the advisory committee process for Title I projects. When Howe left, his Associate Commissioner for Elementary and Secondary Education, Leon Lessinger, who was now leading the traditionalist cause, then made a strenuous attempt to kill the proposed amendment at the Bureau of the Budget. He failed in this effort, but did succeed in alerting the new Finch–Allen forces in DHEW to the issue; they rejected the traditionalist view and gave continued support to the Howe amendment. The amendment ran into trouble in the House, where it was killed by committee conservatives.

However, timely new leadership from Senator Mondale of Minnesota on the Senate side of the Capitol resulted in conferring a new authority on USOE: the 1970 ESEA amendments provided for parental participation to be established locally not only for ESEA Title I, but for other federal programs where such involvement would increase the effectiveness of the program. Under this new authority, USOE can establish criteria for participation by the parents of children affected by programs, and can also establish ground rules for the functioning of the parental advisory process. These new ground rules will provide parental groups with adequate opportunity to present their views on project application before they are submitted for formal approval by state or other authority. The result is that the federal Commissioner of Education has powers to create new avenues of advocacy for the poor in program areas, like vocational education, ESEA Title III, and federally impacted aid, which have historically ignored the special needs of poor children.[3] In a very real sense, the amendment constitutes a spin-off from the client advocacy movement, as reflected in the part played by the parents.

Thus, parent advocacy, as manifested in the two types of involvement described, has been slowly and steadily making inroads into school resistance over the new participation of poor people in their children's education. As the schools were gradually yielding to this level of involvement, the client advocacy movement was gaining momentum and muscle. Poor parents, along with increasingly well-organized community groups, began to escalate their concept of involvement. In this escalation, the demands for power and reform would come to the fore.

The Escalation of Parent Advocacy

As parent and community groups particularly concerned with education moved on the school establishment to gain participation, they were joined by other forces within the community. Among them were the local community action agencies, model cities groups, and civil rights groups, each vying for control over a piece of the school action. When the school establishment resisted, these forces aimed broadsides first at the schools for their failures to educate children, then at their failure to involve the community in planning, and finally at their decisions over the allocation of the new federal educational funds. No longer satisfied with patronizing promises from school authorities to make their programs more "relevant" to their clients, the poor began to march directly on the sources of middle-class power, which were dominating the authority structure. Occurring during the latter 1960's, two thrusts emerged in the parent-community drive for power in the schools, and they were both concerned with governance. One emphasized "community involvement" in the affairs of the school; the other called for organizational "decentralization" of its authority structure. Both thrusts have relied on federal sponsorship and funds, at least in part, for their implementation.

COMMUNITY INVOLVEMENT

The thrust for community involvement has moved rapidly from the stage of limited parent and local advisory committees for federally sponsored projects to the stage of broad demands for major decision-making authority over school programs and the hiring of personnel. As a concept, a trend, or a reality, it cannot be described in the form of any one particular model or pattern. Nevertheless, despite its fluidity and variations, it has identifiable patterns. These evolving patterns of involvement were described in the report of the DHEW Task Force on Urban Education, chaired by Wilson Riles, to Commissioner James E. Allen, Jr., on January 5, 1970. The several patterns also constitute stages of involvement, and are categorized as "participation," "partnership," and "control."

1. As participation is conceived here, with its possible combination of advisory and policy-making functions, there is no
guarantee that community parents and residents would really
have an effective role in the governance over programs in their
local schools. . . .

2. With partnership, described here as a division of authority,
there is a sharing of the decision-making power—either in an
informal arrangement (e.g., a set of understandings worked
out with the local school board and administration) or a formal
agreement (e.g., a legal contract stipulating the precise division of authority and responsibility). . . .

3. With control, conceived here as full authority in fiscal, programmatic, and hiring matters, the community board or authority legally replaces the central school board. Within the
limits of state laws and municipal regulations, including any
other agencies with which it must deal (e.g., the teachers'
union), the community can operate its school or sub-system
making such changes as it deems necessary and can afford.[4]

Viewing these categories as consisting of rungs on a ladder, federal funds and laws supplied the initiative for most of the activities which took place in the schools during the sixties under the
first category of "participation." Having mandated the "advisory
committee" activity under EOA and ESEA, the administering federal agencies then went to work on spelling out the details of this
kind of participation in their guidelines. Frequently, they were
brought in to referee disputes between local groups and the
schools. These conflicts have very often been the signal that local
groups were escalating their demands from the passive stage of
participation to the higher levels of "partnership" and "control."
One fact which came through loud and clear in the local hassles
over the schools was that federal funding and federal guidelines
had created the opportunity for local dissent from the decisions of
school authorities; and the possible interruption in federal funding
was the most compelling reason for the school authorities to listen
to the new sounds of protest.[5]

Moving on to the second rung of the community involvement
ladder, a "sleeper" federal program has been quietly going about

the business of placing poor parents in the driver's seat of their children's educational vehicle. While political controversy has swirled around the parent involvement policies of Head Start and Title I, the Follow Through program is moving the schools into the realm of partnership with the community through model early childhood programs in which parents participate fully in the decision-making process. Follow Through, which picks up the Head Start children at the kindergarten level, has been busy with a whole series of projects which are fundamentally changing education at the early grade levels of the schools. Through agreements negotiated with USOE, the specific contractual forms which the local partnership will take are cemented. A remarkable factor in this development is that the local power-sharing arrangements have been carried on in urban and rural districts in all sections of the country without an audible outcry about a federal effort to take over the operation of school programs.

Among the 140 communities which operated projects in 1969–70, about one-tenth have installed parent control in their program in a variety of ways. In some cases, such as in those projects sponsored by Ira Gordon from the University of Florida, parent-educators are trained first as aides and then as instructors to go into the homes of project children, where they teach parents how to increase the child's intellectual ability as well as to enhance his personal and social development. Other project approaches emphasize the design of program and the control of funds and personnel. Projects which emphasize these radical departures from traditional school practice are found not only in the "likely" places of New York, Philadelphia, and Washington, but also in such "unlikely" non-urban places as Pulaski County, Arkansas; Greeley, Colorado; and Fairfield County, South Carolina. These models are beginning to show promise. For example, the parent-implemented Follow Through program in Pulaski County, Arkansas, has already shown effective results in the first two years it has been in operation. With parents deciding what the program content is to be and how the children are to learn, the project has succeeded in reducing absenteeism among its students by 85 per cent. It has also succeeded in improving the mathematical and reading skills of the project children to the point where second-graders are performing at the level of typical third-graders in the same school.[6]

Another form of the partnership pattern moving toward full control is reflected in experimental model programs. One example of this form is the Anacostia Community School Project functioning in the Anacostia area of Washington, D. C., under a federal USOE grant. In this case, the Anacostia Project represents a cooperative effort on the part of the community, the public schools of the District, and USOE to find and then to disseminate new and effective solutions to the problems confronting urban education. Begun in 1968 with a presidential mandate,[7] the Anacostia Project is to provide an effective and orderly model for decentralization, community involvement, improved educational services, the multiple use of community and cultural resources, and new forms of the community school. In its scope, the project consists of an all-grade eleven-school subsystem in the overcrowded central city. There are approximately 14,000 students involved in the various activities and components of the project. Its governance is carried out through an elective Community School Area Board, composed of teachers, parents, students, and community leaders, which has complete decision-making authority over the federal funds from USOE. Reflecting essentially the same composition, neighborhood advisory boards—one for each school—also perform decision-making functions in conjunction with the area board, such as having a decisive role in the hiring of principals and teachers.

Other features of this partnership model include: the gaining of de facto decision-making involvement by the area board on the use of regular school funds; the development of a sense of cohesiveness between the community and staff; the independent staff–community acquisitions of new sources of funding above and beyond their regular USOE grant—now in excess of $1 million; and the development of new educational and education-related roles for community people.[8] An unexpected test of the partnership power of the Anacostia Project arose in October 1971 when traditionalist research forces within USOE notified the project that federal funds were being withdrawn. Reacting swiftly and vigorously, over 200 angry parents and workers jammed USOE offices and gained a reprieve from Commissioner Sidney P. Marland, Jr., who, following an official appeal from the project, decided to continue funding but under a new set of objectives. Subsequently, the Education Amendments of 1972 transferred the project from USOE to the new National Institute of Education, where its future is uncertain.

On the last rung of the ladder, full control projects of any significance are almost non-existent. While various projects may be termed as fully parent or community-controlled, they are, upon close inspection, almost always variants of the partnership pattern.

Looking beyond the characteristics and achievements of these and other examples as initial steps in the process, it is evident that the federal sponsorship of community involvement is continuing under the ESEA amendments of 1970. Not only have federal funds stimulated involvement, but they have also become a force behind a second process of fostering school authority decentralization.

DECENTRALIZATION

"Decentralization" is a term that evokes a knee-jerk reaction from the usual school administrator who senses that he is about to be dethroned from his seat of near-absolute authority. Since school authority in most states has been reduced to a voluminous legal code, the process of redistributing the power is subject to legislative and executive action at state and local levels. As local groups have moved up the ladder of involvement toward the point of control, they are shifting their ground to that of seeking formal assignments of school authority. Again, the Task Force Report on Urban Education provides a useful classification of the stages of decentralized school authority:

> 1. Decentralization which assigns certain types of administrative matters (e.g., placement of teachers, use of specially trained personnel, processing of requests for materials and equipment) to a geographical subdivision of the school district. . . .

2. Decentralization in which the geographical subdivisions have area or district superintendents who handle all of the above types of matters and also have major authority for programmatic and personnel affairs. . . .

3. Decentralization which permits a *de facto* community involvement in the decision-making process in the form of an advisory board or a planning council for a school or subsystem. . . .

4. Decentralization which involves full delegation of authority and responsibility, including the financial area, to a duly constituted legal entity, such as a nonprofit corporation or another school board within the geographical limits of a school district.[9]

With regard to the decentralization stages described, there are many school systems for which there is no decentralization at all. In some instances, the systems are too small in terms of the numbers of people and school units involved for decentralization to be an issue. However, where sizable systems are involved, the lack of decentralization can either be a case of the clients—parents and students—generally demonstrating acceptance of the educational programs offered, as often exemplified by affluent suburban systems, or it can be a case of the educational establishment having enough "clout" to ward off client attempts to institute decentralization, as in Boston.

On the first rung of the ladder, consisting of routine administrative matters, Chicago affords an example. On the next rung, where administrative power-sharing occurs within levels of the educational establishment, Los Angeles has, for some time, afforded an illustration. In recent years, Philadelphia has begun to accord its area superintendents increased authority and responsibility over program, personnel, and their slice of the funds. On the third rung of the ladder, the de facto community involvement in policymaking through some kind of advisory board, the relationship of the Anacostia Community School Project with the Washington school system affords a convenient example. In this instance, a new administrative unit has come into existence with an administrator who operates within a dualistic chain of command. For certain matters involving regular school system funds, he reports to the superintendent of the main school system; for other matters involving federal and foundation funds, he reports to the community board of the subsystem.

The fourth rung of decentralization, involving full delegation of authority and responsibility—including control over regular state and local monies from a school system's funds on a legal basis, has yet to occur. Thus far, federal funding and authority have not been directly instrumental in the decentralization process, with the exception of the Anacostia Project. True, they have played a facilitating role in that they have generated the involvement of local groups that must precede demands for systems decentralization, but they have not, as yet, mandated the delegation of legally held powers.

It is worth noting, however, that in the most significant instance nationally of legal decentralization, New York City made specific use of the federal funds as a vehicle for decentralization in proposals placed before the legislature of the State of New York in 1968 by the Governor, following recommendations directly received from the Board of Education for New York City and advocated by Mayor John Lindsay. These proposals were aimed at ways to decentralize the colossus of the New York City school system with the clear intent of placing a large measure of school system authority directly in the hands of 33 decentralized boards of education. As city officials watched in agony, the decentralization authority was considerably watered down by the New York State Legislature before final enactment. A provision that remained intact throughout the process, however, was that specially identified federal funds would be the prime target of local decentralized authority. The larger and more regular state and local funds needed to operate the system were kept under the centralized control of the New York City Board of Education. A focal point of contention between the forces of centralized systems control versus neighborhood community control in 1968 was the $75 million Title I prize— with its capability for generating school-based employment and the associated control of staff selection.[10] Subsequently, less sizable amounts of state "urban" funds came along to assist in the process. The avowed purpose of the plan was to empower local boards, in direct response to local advocates, to design innovative programs for educational improvements. The climb to the fourth rung of decentralization is, indeed, a giant step for more than just the educational establishment.

Advocacy for educational reform through the process of assigning either increased de facto powers or recognized legal authority to community groups is, in effect, a federally generated phenomenon. Federal mandates and funds provide the tangible substance— as well as the force—for joining the local conflicts over the governance of the schools. Federal influence, in most instances, has turned in the direction of endorsing the redistribution of the tightly held powers of the educational establishment. And it is likely that the influence will continue to move in this direction. A look at Washington officials under fire gives some indicators as to why this is likely to happen.

USOE Turns in the Direction of Advocacy

By 1968, the client advocacy movement for the poor had not only gained in momentum, numbers, and organizational capability, but it had also developed real leadership with a sense of destiny. In the movement's quest to gain an increased share of the power now held by the establishment, forces within and speaking for the poor began their direct moves in 1968 to enlist the Federal Government's help in hastening the process of power redistribution. These moves were aimed at the top officials of a number of government agencies, among them being the Departments of Labor; Agriculture; Health, Education, and Welfare; and the Office of Economic Opportunity. Thus, federal officialdom came face to face with demands for participation by poor clients—and education was no exception.

COMMISSIONER HOWE AND THE POOR PEOPLE

An impressive display of advocacy for improving the educational services to poor children occurred during the historic Poor

People's Campaign of 1968, which was conceived, conducted, and coordinated by the Southern Christian Leadership Conference. As a part of their summer encampment in Washington and their petitions to all branches of the Federal Government, the representatives of the poor formally presented some very specific demands to the federal end of the educational establishment, namely, DHEW–USOE. For the most part, these demands expressed the desire of poor people to participate more actively than heretofore in the educational decision-making process for their children, but they also focused on a new aspect of their platform, specifically, a direct concern for the proper use of federal funds to serve the poorest children and their schools.

USOE, under the leadership of Commissioner Howe, gave genuinely close attention to the demands of the poor and then formally responded to them. He agreed to review and revise policies to strengthen the poverty thrust of all of USOE's programs—and, in particular, ESEA Title I—in order to achieve an increased funding focus on the needs of the poorest children. In this connection, new policy statements from Howe to the chief state school officers emphasized both the necessity of concentrating Title I funds on these children and of achieving comparability of non-federal expenditures between target and non-target schools.[11] Also, USOE opened its doors a crack wider to the voices of advocacy by making practical arrangements for periodic meetings with representative groups of the poor.

In addition, Howe's attention to these demands resulted in the creation of complaint machinery through which the poor and professionals working in their behalf could now effectively address instances of local non-compliance with the federal requirements. As a part of this machinery, what amounted to a federal bypass of the state and local levels of the educational establishment was created. It now became possible for the client advocates to gain leverage on the local educational situation and the state, by first asking for an investigation of a well-substantiated complaint and then by demanding federal redress. That is, the complaint machinery now involved direct federal contact with the complainant, rather than relying on the traditional route of state referral and routine processing by self-serving state agencies. And through analyses of state-local response to questions derived from local client allegations and documentation of non-compliance, this machinery gave greater substance to the validity of well-documented complaints than before. Howe, indeed, had begun to turn USOE in the direction of client advocacy. And the poor people were quick to seize the opportunity offered by this change in direction.

Leaders of the Poor People's Campaign concerned with education pushed vigorously on the front of local confrontations over the use of ESEA Title I funds. Particular scrutiny was given in 1968 and 1969 to situations in the South, where local school administrators since the inception of Title I had consistently excluded poor people from the decisions on allocations of funds. This scrutiny soon revealed that these administrators were also pursuing policies which subverted the federal regulations on several counts: using funds to serve non-poor children with Title I services, following traditional rather than innovative routes in serving the poor, and violating federal rules on involving the poor.

As the grounds for complaint actions in the South began to emerge more sharply following the demands of the Poor People and the Howe response, the competence to deal with the complaint process was also to develop. In Mississippi, the Delta Ministry (acting under the sponsorship of the National Council of Churches) joined forces with the Legal Defence and Educational Fund of the NAACP to aid poor people in correcting local abuses of Title I funding. Legal services became available from law firms supported locally by the OEO legal services division which, in turn, joined the cooperative effort. Some dedicated professional talent was now aiding less-schooled poor people to develop the process of client advocacy by steering them through the nitty-gritty of documenting local project expenditures.

The tactics of the Poor People's Campaign for the complaint process were direct and to the point. Reinforced by legal expertise, local poor people first sought information from local school superintendents from their Title I project files. If refused access to the files, the poor invoked federal regulations which guaranteed such access and forced open the files. And, if necessary, they went to

USOE in Washington to do it. This process in itself forced a new federal guide in the spring of 1969 which guaranteed local groups the right to one photocopy of each Title I document in the local files.[12] Once local poor people obtained precise dollar information on the allocation of funds, they prepared detailed accounts of how these expenditures violated the federal requirements serving target area schools and for meeting the most pressing needs of poor children. Legal experts, working with the poor, converted these statements into formal complaints, following federal format and procedures. They then filed these complaints directly with USOE in Washington. And by the end of 1968, the process was in full sway. However, the first major test of both the complaint machinery and USOE's advocacy in behalf of poor clients came from Mississippi—after Howe had left USOE with the change of administrations.

USOE AND COMPLIANCE ISSUES IN MISSISSIPPI

Beginning in December 1968, USOE received written complaints on 12 Mississippi Title I programs, plus allegations of statewide violations, all of which established a definite pattern of non-compliance. In the Mississippi instances, the charges were specific as to the local agency, the target schools, Title I projects and the details of violations—giving citations as to amounts of money, timing, and supporting data—all related to the USOE guidelines. In addition, corroborating information was also arriving from testimony given by state and local witnesses in court cases involving desegregation, as the Legal Defense and Educational attorneys expertly questioned local school officials on their practices involving federal funds. The questioning of witnesses revealed that the fund's attorneys were far ahead of the superintendents in their understanding of the federal law and its regulations.

Invoking the complaint machinery established by Howe, USOE, for the first time in its history, took on the task of investigating a state's integrity in administering federal funds, since the Mississippi complaints had blazed a trail of allegations that led straight to the door of the State Superintendent of Public Instruction and

his staff. On June 23, 1969, Commissioner James Allen informed
Garvin H. Johnston, the Mississippi Superintendent, of the USOE
concern over the complaints and called for a full review of the state
program. On July 1, 1969, the formal review process began with a
visit to Jackson, Mississippi, by a team of five USOE staff members
headed by the Director of the Division of Compensatory Education. Interrogations of state officials, reviews of state files, and interviews with parents and local supporters of the poor quickly
established clear patterns of violations on the local use of funds.
Violations included the use of federal funds to replace local funds
in the target schools, the excessive use of funds for capital outlay
purposes, the use of federal funds to maintain segregated schools,
and the use of funds to serve non-target schools and children.[13]

A high point of the July 1–3 review was a meeting in Jackson
with parents and representatives of poor people. State officials were
very reluctant to attend this meeting held in their own offices, and
finally agreed only to sit in as observers. It was very evident that
they were nervous at the prospect of facing dissatisfied poor con-
stituents and would have greatly preferred to avoid it completely.
In fact, they declined to attend the meeting at all if "civil rights
lawyers" were to be present, in view of pending court actions
against several state officials. Some 15 parents, who came to two
sessions on July 2, told the federal team of their frustrations in
gaining access to local officials dispensing Title I funds; and they
also gave tearful testimony about the plight of their children. Typical comments spoke of the harshness of the schools in denying adequate food and clothing services to the children, while the schools
were loading up their storerooms with gadgetry and their classrooms with band instruments for children, regardless of their musi-
cal inclinations. State officials listened with stoney faces and spoke
only to request the names—and proper spelling—of persons giving
testimony, as a means of "reassuring" the witnesses of the state's
concern.

Following their reviews, the federal team met with State Superintendent Johnston and state officials regarding their findings. In
this exit interview on July 3, the State Superintendent was informed
of the serious nature of the Mississippi violations and was advised

that major changes would be needed to avert a formal hearing to decide on whether Title I funds should be cut off from the state. A picture of injured innocence, the Superintendent assured the team that Mississippi wished to abide by the law and all USOE regulations, and, if necessary, they would change their procedure in order not to jeopardize the $40 million in federal funds coming into the state. If the state was a bit slow to get the message on the reform mandate of Title I, it was quick to catch the point of a loss of federal funds. Southern schoolmen have a saying that "the only sin worse than integration is the loss of federal money"—and Johnston was about to demonstrate his virtue.

When Commissioner Allen wrote to Johnston on July 9, 1969, he advised him that Mississippi applications for the new fiscal year were not to be approved until the state corrected glaring weaknesses in its programs; in effect, Allen withdrew the federal funds pending compliance with federal demands. He also stipulated that local visits would be made by federal teams to some 20 communities to verify tentative findings of non-compliance. Johnston was asked to revise state practices promptly and to call a meeting of the local superintendents during July to inform them of the necessary changes. The State Superintendent speedily complied with all the federal requests.

Further USOE team visits to the Mississippi communities verified the accuracy of the tentative findings of non-compliance, and added to the case against the state. Investigators found that Title I money was being used by the Mississippi schools as a belated and ineffective "equalizer" of services in the target schools and that local officials were ignoring most Title I requirements—partly because of ignorance of them and partly because of indifference toward them. Also, USOE kept Mississippi on the hook for further compliance; and, in August 1969, the state was told to proceed with portions of applications dealing only with health, welfare, nutritional, and instructional services to children. Allen additionally insisted on new reporting procedures for establishing the "comparability" of local expenditures between non-target and target schools, and required this comparability to be achieved by September 1970, rather than by September 1971 as proposed by Johnston.[14]

USOE's experience with Mississippi was to lead to larger events. For the first time in the recollection of USOE staff, the Office had taken strict "withholding" measures to enforce its own policies. And it was led to this course of action against a state whose record of defiance of federal orders was legion. Previous efforts to achieve compliance had either taken the peaceful route of negotiation to greater adherence or had secured the promise to do so from erring states found in violation of rules to obtain their cooperation. Mississippi had so abused these assurances as to make USOE's corrective measures a necessity. Having corralled Mississippi, USOE was faced with the necessity of national enforcement of its policies in the face of widespread complaints over the misuse of funds. Indeed, USOE could not afford to single out Mississippi for punitive action in the face of an obvious southern attitude of "we are only doing what others are doing."

USOE'S DILEMMA ON CLIENT ADVOCACY

By early 1970, USOE had found itself perched on a precarious ledge. On the one hand, the Office, never a strong agency, was being seriously weakened by the sliding education priority and the erosion of Allen's authority within the Nixon Administration on policies dealing with school desegregation. Moreover, USOE was now in the spotlight to enforce its own policies, and was now vulnerable to attack because of promulgating policies which it did not enforce. On the other hand, USOE was being publicly challenged to enforce strong Title I policies which would require more—not less—strength than it had possessed in the past. Coming in strongly on the side of the Title I change-advocate position was the Senate Labor and Public Welfare Committee's Report of January 1970, which stressed the need for the "monitoring function to be performed so that all states are subject to continuing review on the effectiveness of the (Title I) program in meeting the special needs of poor children within each state."[15]

Even if its diminished strength is increased, which now seems likely under Allen's successor, Sidney Marland, USOE faces another problem that is broader than the one created by the clash of the client advocacy movement with the educational establishment over compliance with Title I policies. In a very real sense, this latter problem—like the one with Title I enforcement—has been posed by the client advocacy movement. Specifically, it is whether in a showdown between school officials empowered to make judgments on educational programs and a client group charging denial of benefits, USOE will really take the side of the clients against the system. Since USOE's orientation traditionally has strictly been that of an ally of its own establishment—the school system—the problem is, indeed, a genuine one. Now USOE finds that a beneficiary group of that system is seeking its advocacy against the system for failure to provide adequate educational services. Since the issues that provide the cause for conflict are embedded in the quality of local educational services, not to mention the judgments of local officials in designing the projects, USOE is being coerced into an intervention in the school process that is already beginning to shatter the peaceful façade of its relations with the states.

A traditional resolution of this problem would bring an automatic referral of responsibility to the states. However, the new forces of advocacy pressing on USOE will undoubtedly demand an examination of the local delivery on a federal commitment involving the educational outcomes for and, therefore, the lifetime expectancies of some eight million beneficiary children. And, indeed, USOE has been edging its way into developing a new institutional stance toward these clients. Whether or not USOE will go the distance and really form a major alliance with them remains to be seen. However, the fact that USOE now faces this dilemma is one legacy of the opportunity strategy for education. The other legacies will be examined next, as the transition to the proposals being made for a new national strategy for education.

7

From Partial Strategies
to a Full Strategy

THE NATIONAL EXPERIENCE WITH PUBLIC EDUCATION in the latter 1960's has painfully demonstrated just how far apart its operating reality has actually been from its political mythology. In the early 1970's, the demand for major system reform in the areas of finance, governance, and program has reached national proportions. But there is no accompanying comprehensive plan or strategy on the horizon that offers the required resources and the necessary leverage to accomplish the reform that is needed for the millions of clients to be served and for the well-being of the nation as a whole. Instead, there is a bleak picture of public education beset with the harsh reality of major problems and encumbered with a mythology that obstructs the development of a national plan for their solution. Therefore, it is within this admixture of reality and mythology that the outcomes of the national experience with public education in the latter 1960's must be interpreted, if a new and complete strategy for education in the 1970's is ever to be successfully formulated and implemented. Accordingly, this chapter begins by examining the two "partial" strategies that surfaced in the Elementary and Secondary Education Act of 1965 as reflective of both the mythology and the realities at the federal, state, and local levels.

Two Partial Strategies

Before the enactment of ESEA in 1965, the political mythology surrounding education—as a function that belonged to the states by virtue of its lack of mention in the Constitution—had led to only a small-scale federal involvement. Principally because of the mythology, the federal involvement in education had been limited to specific categorical programs designed to serve a strategy other than education, such as national defense, agricultural development, scientific development, or the alleviation of poverty. One result had been a laborious pile of piecemeal federal categorical programs in which education had generally performed as a service to other strategies, rather than being regarded as worthy of a strategy in and of itself. A more important result is that education had never been regarded, from the vantage point of the Federal Government, in terms of its potential for the realization of long-range societal goals for equality of opportunity or for maximum achievement for all of our people. In 1965, however, the Federal Government started edging in the direction of a strategy for education—even if implicitly—with the enactment of ESEA. Through ESEA, education acquired the status of a partial strategy in the federal structure. In acquiring this status, ESEA actually contained not one but two partial strategies, and each acknowledged the political mythology and the operating realities as perceived at that time.

One of these partial strategies was ESEA's massive Title I which was incorporated as a main—albeit ambivalent—component of the opportunity strategy by the Johnson Administration planners. Unlike many other programs of the opportunity strategy which went directly to local agencies, Title I went through the states on the way to the local schools serving children from low-income families. Also, while the formula identified a poverty target population which was clearly the same population to be served by other programs of the opportunity strategy, the statement of Title I's intent was ambiguous as between aiding the system and helping the clients. Moreover, the Title I mandate, which specified the need for special educational services to be provided in recognition of the special needs of the target population, conferred upon the states the authority and responsibility for decision-making on the services to be provided. However, the ambivalence was not alone in making Title I a partial, or incomplete, strategy. What it lacked as a full strategy were the mechanisms for carrying out the mission once it was defined and the resources to accomplish that mission once the mechanisms were designed.

Like the ambivalence, these lacks were compounded out of political mythology and the educational underestimation of the magnitude of the task involved, including the resources that would be needed. The implicit assumptions underlying Title I as a strategy revealed the political mythology in that (1) the states should—and could—control the program, and (2) the state and local establishments knew how to serve the needs of the target poverty population. In turn, the second political assumption revealed a third one at the level of the system itself; specifically, that the process of education for the middle-class child would suit the poverty child. The operating reality within education was recognized in that (1) the target poverty group did need special educational services, and (2) the schools needed additional monies with which to provide such services. Title I was, indeed, a mixture of mythology, reality, and underestimation. And it didn't work.

By the close of the 1960's, the three political assumptions were in a shambles, and the real problems being faced by the schools were steadily escalating. Specifically, an intensified middle-class program for the poverty child had proved a failure in the academic program areas, and only in the education-related areas, such as health and nutrition, was there any noticeable payoff. The failure clearly demonstrated that, by and large, the professional establishment was not knowledgeable about serving the needs of this target population. And the states had revealed that claiming control over education was very different from actually exerting control over it. Even as the evidence of the failure mounted, there was no adequate governmental leverage to correct the system deficiencies at the state and local levels that had produced the failure; USOE lacked the clout. What the failure had demonstrated was the lack of adequate mechanisms for creating the social change which the opportunity strategy was seeking to place in motion. The educational system had revealed itself to be powerful enough to resist the limited force for social change even when ESEA Title I was coupled with the other titles of the act, reinforced by the community action thrust of the Economic Opportunity Act, and pressured by the desegregation thrust of the Civil Rights Act. As the deep-seated problems that existed in the areas of governance and program became increasingly delineated, the problems in the financial areas steadily mounted. ESEA Title I, as a partial strategy and the main education component of the opportunity strategy, had fallen short of the mark.

The other partial strategy within ESEA fared no better. This strategy, which was made up of the five initial titles comprising ESEA, carried the thrust of securing institution-initiated improvement by means of the selective application of resources at critical junctures within the system, that is, the special educational needs of poverty children (I), new learning materials (II), provision of new informational inputs through innovation and research (III and IV), and the strengthening of state-level administrative agencies (V). Thus, although ESEA identified key areas of change, it failed to provide adequate resources for dealing with these changes. Even more decisively, ESEA failed to provide the kinds of mechanisms that would bring about the changes through applying appropriate pressures at the state and local governance levels. The key political—and educational—assumption behind this partial strategy was that the schools knew what to do and merely needed the resources with which to do it. While real problems had been recognized in the identification of key areas, underestimation of the magnitude of these problems was apparent in the level of resources provided and in the lack of adequate mechanisms for leverage.

By the close of the 1960's, the reasoning behind the other partial strategy within ESEA had also proven fallacious. Instead of initiating internal improvements on the way to institutional reforms, this strategy had merely embellished public education with the same unresponsive and inappropriate symbolism that had failed to deliver in the past, and had also encouraged some new administrative tactics for maintaining existing inequities, like supplanting. Thus, both strategies within ESEA had fallen well short of their primary goals—the rescue of the children of poverty and the improvement of the institution that was expected to perform the rescue. As the failure to reach these goals became increasingly apparent, there was a corresponding realization that the political mythology and perceived realities, which had produced the solutions of ESEA in the mid-sixties, were faulty as well. By 1969, it was apparent that the educational systems needed more than money if they were going to contribute substantively to breaking the poverty cycle and to achieving an acceptable level of performance for all of their clients, including the poor ones. There were also other outcomes from the experience with the partial strategies of ESEA in the latter 1960's.

Outcomes of the Two Partial Strategies

The experience with the two partial strategies of ESEA in the 1960's has produced a documentation of the problems and needs of public education in delivering on its mission of providing a full educational opportunity for all of its clients. This documentation consists of a set of outcomes—some of which have already been analyzed for their significance—that are, in actuality, by products of the experience. When these additional outcomes are examined in the light of their blending of political mythology and broad social reality, they afford the bridge to a new strategy.

While the problems of poverty and discrimination had always been a part of the national picture, the decade of the sixties brought the revelation of their depth and complexity, which, in turn, produced another revelation: These problems would not be resolved with partial mechanisms for redress and limited resources. The thrust to overcome poverty and discrimination had not resulted in the solution of the problems, but it had resulted in a by-product— the illumination of the extent to which the inequities and injustices represented by the problems were being generally sanctioned by the nation and maintained through its social institutions. In other words, despite its political mythology, America was, in reality, the land of opportunity only for some of its citizens, but not for all of them. Moreover, it was apparent that those citizens who possessed a clear right-of-way to this opportunity were in no hurry, if not downright unwilling, to share it with those who did not. Those citizens for whom this access to opportunity had been blocked soon began to demand an instant and total right-of-way to it via the same institutions that had been providing that opportunity to more favored citizens.

Inevitably, education became a prime target of this demand as the well-advertised pathway to a full and productive life for all citizens. That the pathway was only a myth for the poverty—and often minority—child was soon well documented as the facts and figures began accumulating on public education's general treatment of him. Indeed, before the implementation of the partial strategies of ESEA, the documentation for the War on Poverty had clearly revealed that the poverty child was getting approximately the same program—although usually diluted in terms of specific services and overall quality—as his economically favored counterpart. Despite the demonstration of the program's inappropriateness for the poverty child through such means as his lowered achievement level and attendance rate, it was further revealed that this state of affairs had been going on for years without any systematic efforts at either the state or local governance levels to correct it.

Nevertheless, the pathway-for-all myth continued to have political potency when it was combined with another myth—that the schools really knew what to do for the poverty child; all that was needed was money. With the arrival of the two partial strategies of ESEA, the myth of money as the answer was put to the test, although the other myth was clearly involved. And, as the sixties drew to a close, it was apparent that virtually all of the school systems had failed the test. In failing it, the systems had revealed a lot about themselves to a whole lot of people, including their poverty clients. One revelation was that the schools really did not know the poverty child and his needs. As the schools slowly began to address themselves to the impact on the educative process of such basic human needs as health, nutrition, clothing, and family support, it became apparent that the resources and services being provided were inadequate for the task of compensating for an unfavorable environment outside the school. A second revelation was the exposure to view of several unstated premises that had worked against the poverty child, such as the main burden of success in the program being placed on the child rather than on the school (with the result that the poverty child was being viewed as the deficient child), the provision of access to some kind of opportunity being enough, and the middle-class program beamed at the hypothetical average child (IQ between 90 and 110 and reading at grade level) being the right program. A third revelation was the lack of commitment to—and the absence of—a systematic plan for dealing with the target group of children who had been specifically identified by ESEA Title I for special services. When the intensification approach failed, there was no other major alternative that could be implemented; the second partial strategy within ESEA, self-initiated program improvements within public education, had nothing substantive to offer. It had only reinforced the extant symbolism and practices underlying the intensification approach.

Instead of achieving its missions, ESEA had produced, through its two partial strategies, an irrefutable documentation of the gap between education's mythology and its reality. By 1969, the capacity and the capability of state and local governance levels to design and implement the kinds of improvements that would result in the provision of an equal educational opportunity to all clients, given sufficient resources, had been exploded as myth. In its stead was the reality of a defensive establishment of school administrators which not only was financially close to bankruptcy, but was revealing its bankruptcy in the areas of governance and program as well. For the partial strategies of ESEA to have worked, the myths surrounding education would have had to be proved true, rather than false. Thus, one by-product outcome from ESEA was to dissipate much of the political potency of the time-honored mythology through which public education had succeeded in avoiding its major responsibility for serving all of its clients with effective programs in terms of their needs.

In the other outcomes that also revealed the problems and needs of public education, the partial strategy represented by ESEA Title I, in combination with the programs emanating from the Economic Opportunity Act and the Civil Rights Act, played a prominent role. In singling out the poor for special educational attention through the target population concept, ESEA Title I had opened the door for the poor people to seek redress of the inequities and injustices which education had perpetrated on them, and was now perpetrating on their children. Once the poor people realized that the door was open, they started to push through it with increasingly improved tactics for gaining leverage on the educational system. Expressing resentment and bitterness about the kinds of programs that were being offered to their children, as well as rejecting the deficient child syndrome imposed upon them by the system, they soon realized that merely serving in supportive and advisory roles controlled by the system were insufficient to the changes required. Acquiring expertise on their own and assisted by professionals largely from outside the system, the poor people went to the heart of the matter—the redistribution of administrative decision-making authority, including the use of the federal funds being pumped into the schools on their behalf. In this process, the child "beneficiary" concept implicit in Title I's legislation and the belated program guidelines provided the poor and their advocates with at least some leverage on the school systems. Specifically, the poor were able to assert (1) a demand for system performance in the form of appropriate programs for their children, and (2) a demand for the system to account for the funds that it received in their behalf.

When these Title I leverage mechanisms were coupled with those afforded by the community action thrust under the Economic Opportunity Act, Title VI of the Civil Rights Act, and usually outside-of-education professional expertise, the poor people could ameliorate the situation to some extent, but they still could not redress it. Only when the courts interceded or the federal administrative level stepped in—often gingerly—on behalf of the clients did any major changes occur in the local educational settings; effective state-level intervention was a rare occurrence. What the client advocacy movement revealed was that mechanisms at the local level alone were insufficient against a rigid administrative system that was intent upon maintaining its own ways of doing business.

Thus, while the client advocacy movement in the educational sphere has not succeeded in achieving sufficient leverage on the existing governance of public education to effect adequate program reforms, it has, nevertheless, demonstrated both the magnitude and the kinds of leverage needed, if genuine program reforms are ever to be achieved that will include all of the clients to be served. In so doing, the client advocacy movement has forced a reopening of the issue of educational accountability in the key areas of program and governance by virtue of the default of existing administrative arrangements to provide appropriate programs for the poverty clients. The myth of educational accountability in terms of providing appropriate programs for all clients has given way to the reality of major problems within the system that have been blocking this accountability from being realized for large numbers of clients.

Another outcome has consisted of a set of rising expectations or success-oriented values on the part of poor and minority groups concerning their capabilities for educational performance. They have now set their sights on education—all the way from preschool to graduate school—as their pathway to economic and social success, just as it has always been the pathway in the past for the middle class. Having learned that the system has cheated them for generations, they have now demanded immediate redress of inequities and prompt delivery of full system performance. The realities of gradualism as a measure of progress within our educational system have been neither understood nor accepted by the poor as a satisfactory response to their demand for instant equality of opportunity, and the inability to deliver on these expectations has merely intensified the gulf of misunderstanding that must be bridged between the poor and the affluent society.

Also, the affluent society has further complicated the problem by some general responses of its own. One response has been the successful resistance to the integration approach to achieving equality of educational opportunity of white middle-class groups, either by retreating to the suburbs or by exerting their power within the cities to hold this thrust to mere tokenism. The poor—and particularly the black and Spanish-speaking populations in the cities—have, in turn, countered by seeking control over their neighborhood schools with the argument, "Give us the school and we will provide the quality." Another response has been a growing middle-class refusal to accept fiscal responsibility for school systems, under pressure from poor and minority groups, by voter rejection of tax and bond issues. One other response of the middle class has been to create within their suburban bastions high-quality educational systems, which they both control and support. The insistence of delivery on expectations has thus typically characterized the suburban systems, since the middle-class groups have generally achieved and maintained client accountability and control. But the now comparable insistence by poor and minority groups has proved to be a different matter altogether. Clearly recognizing the point, these groups have increasingly appealed to the Federal Government and to the courts for delivery on their expectations. In so doing, the clients have contributed to the development of a new and active federal role with regard to public education—another outcome of the experience with the two partial strategies of the 1960's.

The emerging federal role has also been stimulated by the general inability of the state and local administrative levels to deliver on the opportunities afforded to them by the program funds and thrusts of the two strategies embedded within ESEA. That is, the development of this new role accelerated, as the inequities at the state and local levels were illuminated and as these levels of the establishment showed little inclination toward or concrete plans for change. Accordingly, in an effort to establish the ground rules for instituting innovations and leverage mechanisms, as well as to prevent further attrition of such opportunities, the federal involvement veered in the direction of client advocacy through such tactics as the Title I guidelines dealing with comparability, concentration, and parent advisory committees, and the creation of a direct federal appeal mechanism for the clients. Veering in this direction has not been an easy task since the federal administrative level and the Congress have typically been in close alliance with the educational establishments at the state and local levels. But the realization of the magnitude of the existing inequities—coupled with the inabilities of the educational system at the state and local levels to carry out major changes in the critical areas of finance, governance, and program—have necessitated an active federal involvement on behalf of the clients.

For quite different reasons, the educational establishments at both the state and local levels have also contributed to the development of an increasingly active federal role. First, the abuses of the monies received from the various ESEA titles have forced the Federal Government into initiating administrative and legal corrective measures in line with federal legislation and guidelines. In turn, these fiscal abuses and necessary corrective actions have spilled over into the program and governance areas as well, since fiscal abuses led to the exposures of inequities in all areas of the educational enterprise. And these revelations have led to a growing public demand for the reform in the key areas of public education, which has now included the middle-class clients as well.

At the same time that the abuses, corrective actions, existing inequities, and client pressures were gaining momentum, most local school districts, with the exception of the affluent suburban ones, were confronting deepening financial crises. Although not attributable to the partial education strategies of ESEA, the financial crisis now permeating almost all of education has constituted a prime reason for increased federal involvement. State and local resources have proved inadequate to meet the needs of all of the clients. For example, in response to the fiscal crisis that is closing in on them, some of the major urban school systems are moving toward novel solutions which have led first to their state capitals and then inevitably to Washington for signs of relief. As one approach to the problem of bankruptcy, Detroit sued the State of Michigan unsuccessfully for funds needed to provide "equal education" in that city. In the face of this rebuff, on May 12, 1970, Norman Drachler, Detroit's able superintendent, told the Senate Select Committee on Equal Educational Opportunity that the only remaining hope for financing education was the Federal Government:

> It is my personal view that public education as constituted today, is incapable as a state-controlled responsibility to meet the challenges of the coming decades. The Federal Government must assume a major responsibility for the future of pub-

lic education. It is the only agency that can tap the nation's human and financial resources capable of assessing and performing the tasks ahead. We simply do not have the time for 50 different State agencies to struggle with the issue independently. Ours is a mobile and impatient society. Ignorance cannot be quarantined nor tolerated.

I am not worried about Federal control or a centrally dominated educational institution. We are a pragmatic people and with the transition of responsibility we can develop procedures and processes that can bring about much greater local influence and control upon education than we think we have had in the past. We have demonstrated, in the past, a talent for preserving idealogic principles while devising pragmatic means to adjust to new conditions. We can do so again.[1]

Some 16 months later, before the same Senate Committee, Philadelphia's Superintendent Mark Shedd was to state the case for federal rescue in even more desperate terms. Citing the worsening financial condition of the city school system as a result of state and local default in meeting its needs, Shedd proposed the full "nationalization" of the large city school systems.[2]

Thus, progressive leaders of the system have themselves come to the realization that their only remaining hope for the system's rescue is the Federal Government. In strict financial terms, only the federal level has access to the resources now needed to bail out the system and its clients; the states simply lack the means to equalize the system and, then, to fund its deficits. Federal intervention in the governance area is fast becoming an accepted necessity to bring about desegregation of the system, as well as to direct its attention to a priority national need—the provision of equality of opportunity. Furthermore, state officials and legislatures are increasingly deferring to the federal level as the source of governmental revenues and power to enable the system to function. As the financial crisis deepens and the pressure for reform increases, anguished cries about federal control of education have practically vanished from the political scene in Washington. In their stead is a search for federal solutions and an accompanying readiness for federal leadership.

What both the search and the readiness for solutions must pro-

duce is a strategy that will result in the renewal, reform, and re-
financing of American public education if the millions of clients
are to be provided with a genuine equality of opportunity. Education is not deferrable any longer—if, indeed, it ever has been. The
partial strategies embedded within ESEA—with their limited
funds, incomplete mechanisms for renewal and reform, and uneasy
mixture of mythology and reality—have fallen short of achieving
their goals. But, in so doing, these partial strategies have illuminated not only the need for a new and complete strategy but also
what the main premises of this strategy for the seventies and beyond must be.

Premises for the National Strategy

The first of the proposed premises is that the strategy must elevate education to the fully acknowledged status of a basic human
right. Previous concepts of education—as a privilege granted by
society, of the provision of access to some kind of opportunity being sufficient, of the main burden of securing this opportunity
resting upon the individual—must be discarded. They must be
replaced by a strategy that translates education as a basic human
right into a purpose designed to provide a genuinely equal and
adequate set of educational services to all Americans, so as to assure their ability to function effectively in the society. In addition,
the strategy must assert that the protection, under the law, of education as a basic human right of each citizen is a national obliga-
tion.

The second premise proposed is that the strategy must be enacted into law by the Congress. In this connection, the strategy
must encompass all persons and must be on a scale of resources
sufficient to accomplish its purpose over time. What this premise
means is that the strategy must address the needs of the clients
from preschool through adult education, at all levels of the system,
and for all groups to be served by it. For a strategy of this magnitude, the time factors for implementation are important. Therefore,
it is further proposed that the decade of the 1970's will be required
for the full implementation of the strategy, with adaptations being

made as needed in the future to meet the changing requirements of the population.

The third premise is that the strategy, as translated into legislation, must contain a set of clearly defined tactics through which its purpose can be achieved. These tactics must address the three key areas of the educational enterprise—finance, governance, and program. In combination, they must guarantee to each client accountability and performance by the system on his behalf.

The fourth is that the Federal Government must assume the dominant role in the strategy. As the agency which has assumed the major responsibility for assuring the rights of individuals in the areas of civil rights, voting, welfare, health, and housing, it can do no less in the field of education in view of the default by the states.

The fifth premise is that the strategy must be realistically designed to gain political acceptability in terms of its provisions and the administrative capabilities for its implementation. Political acceptability, in this instance, includes the readiness of, and the timing for, key forces to support the strategy's purpose and legislative proposals.

Thus, this set of five premises is offered as the basis from which the development of a complete national strategy for education can logically proceed. Derived from the problems and the experience of the sixties with the strategies that failed to achieve their goals, these premises permit the articulation of a new strategy in the form of legislative proposals which are solution-oriented for the clients, the public education system, and the nation as a whole. It is this task that is addressed in Part Two: the setting forth of a fully developed national strategy for education appropriate to our national needs during the decade of the 1970's and beyond.

PART TWO
A New National Strategy for the 1970's

8

The Education Mandate

THE FIVE PREMISES REQUISITE FOR THE FULL REALIZATION of a national strategy for education embrace the elevation of education to the fully acknowledged status of a human right, the translation of that right into a legislative mandate, and the assignment of a dominant role in the strategy to the Federal Government. In this chapter we address these premises with main emphasis being given to a description of two key elements of the legislative mandate which would enable the Federal Government to fulfill its assigned role in the attainment of these premises: One is the set of educational guarantees to be made to each American citizen, stated as a bill of rights with a supporting rationale; the other, the federal funding formula necessary to meet individual client needs. The need and national priority for education are interwoven as a part of the presentation of the legislative proposals. We begin with the key substantive element of the legislative proposal and the strategy—the elevation of education to the status of a basic human right.

Education—A Basic Human Right

Three assumptions undergird the rationale presented in support of the proposed bill of rights to establish education as a basic human right through the legislative process. One assumption is that the task of educating all of our citizens must be viewed as a matter of fundamental national policy. Our national goals of social justice, economic progress, and an enlightened citizenry cannot be achieved under a decentralized educational system which permits genuinely equal educational opportunity to be offered only to some,

149

but not to all, of our citizens. A second is that only a firm national legislative commitment that elevates equal educational opportunity to the level of a human right and insists on its fulfillment will accomplish the national policy and goals. An education strategy to carry out this commitment will be successful only to the extent that it defines the national policy in terms of a genuinely equal educational opportunity, clearly identifies the clients to be served—including those needing special assistance, mandates delivery on this policy, and then consistently follows through on the policy over time. The third assumption is that only the Federal Government, at this time in our national history, possesses the power and has the access to the resources which can insure the delivery of a genuinely equal opportunity for education. Just as the Federal Government finally had to legislate to guarantee individual voting rights and to enforce school desegregation, so also will it have to act affirmatively to guarantee the right to an equal education. Thus, the legislative proposal in support of a national strategy of education assigns a key role to the Federal Government for its accomplishment. From these assumptions, both the rationale and its translation into an education bill of rights logically follow.

RATIONALE

Education in the highly technological and rapidly changing American society is an absolute necessity. Without an adequate education, an individual will be impaired in his functioning as a self-respecting, productive human being and a constructive citizen. The concept of education as the privilege of a comparative few might still be justified for a society characterized by the lack of a democratic heritage, insufficient resources, or a lack of sophisticated technology. But it is completely unjustifiable in the American society. The twin rationalizations that the mere provision of access to some kind of educational opportunity is sufficient and that the main burden of responsibility rests with the individual to gain access to this opportunity, whatever it may be, are equally unjustifiable. They have resulted in a series of discriminatory educational practices for which we are now reaping a harvest of bitterness on the part of both the poor and the non-poor alike. Also, they have allowed the schools to engage in the practice of offering educational programs to their clients on a "sink or swim" basis; and, in so doing, the schools have avoided their responsibility for substantively adjusting their programs to meet the varying individual needs of their clients. It is unconscionable, as well as nationally dangerous, to allow the practices resulting from this pair of rationalizations and their attendant bitterness to continue without taking positive action to deal with them. This action is required as a matter of seeing to it that a public trust is discharged in the national interest.

While it is essential that a valid education be provided for all of our citizens, the poor among them must receive special consideration. Education is imperative as a constructive, preventive measure for avoiding the increasingly crushing costs—both economic and human—of economic dependency and racial/ethnic discrimination to the nation as a whole. As an investment approach to breaking the poverty cycle, it holds out the potential for providing the pathway to economic relief for the nation and to productive lives with dignity for all of its citizens. It is no longer acceptable—if, indeed, it ever was—to allow the accidents of either geography or local tradition to deny adequate educational benefits to poor children. Education must become the universally valid passport from poverty to an improved and productive way of life, and it should not be denied to a child because he is born a black in Harlem, a migrant in south Texas, a poor white in Appalachia, or a rural child of poverty in the Mississippi delta.

The schools, like other public social institutions, are financed with public funds for the express purpose of providing important needed services to citizens, as a means of achieving a particular goal that the society defines as being important to its orderly continuation and to its maintenance of values. However, unlike other public social institutions, the services the schools provide must be accepted by our citizens, unless they have the economic means to pay on a private basis for those services elsewhere—it's a matter of law. Also, unlike other public services, the schools require the presence of our citizens as clients beginning at an early age and continuing over long periods of time on a regular basis, whether the

particular citizen in question finds that the services being provided
do or do not meet his particular educational needs. In effect, the
schools are providing a mandatory public service with public
funds to a captive audience of citizens during the critical formative
years of their lives. These conditions—mandatory service, captive
audience, time span, and lack of educational options—have permitted the schools to be increasingly less accountable not only to
some but actually to all of our citizens. As these conditions have
made a citizen accountable to the school in the sense of its having
the right to command his presence for instruction, they make it imperative for him to have the right to demand that the school be
accountable to him through offering him an appropriate and reasonable program for his needs. The effects which an inappropriate
or unreasonable program may have on our young citizens are often
beyond the capability of their parents to counterbalance or the
school to correct. Thus, it becomes imperative that the accountability of the public education institution to its clients be legalized
in order to protect each individual and his educative process and
to insure the adequate discharge of a public trust using public
funds.

Education is a major public institution charged with preparing
our citizenry with the many kinds of knowledge required for
contributing constructively to our nation's continued growth and
development. However, it has lacked both the status and the resources that should be associated with such an important goal. The
main point here is not to analyze the causes which have led to
education's lack, but rather to underscore the urgency of taking
affirmative action to overcome this lack now. The urgency is compounded not only from specific conditions, such as impending
financial breakdown of school systems, disaffected youth—poor
and non-poor alike, and generally unresponsive state and local decisions in the program area, but also from the general context of
major social change brought on by an accelerating technology and
the knowledge explosion. As a nation, our development has been,
and is, phenomenal, but many of our institutions have not kept
pace—and one of them is education. With its particular goal, education must be in the forefront in preparing our citizens to meet

this change in intelligent and productive ways; it is our lien on the future. As a matter of national policy, education must be transformed into the kind of major public institution that will insure this future through clearly defined goals, a broadened social role, and adequate financing on a continuing basis. Any other alternative presents incalculable risks.

To accomplish its goal, education must be recognized as a distinct national priority in and of itself—a priority that does not veer and tack according to the political vicissitudes of each successive administration and of other national priorities. In short, education's priority must have a recognizable identity, and it must become a constant in the national scheme of things. The typical view of the educative process as merely the means to other ends—such as economic well-being and social status, important as these ends are in our society—only addresses a part of education's purpose in a democracy. The other part of this purpose is that the educative process constitutes an end in itself because of its thrusts for rationality, inquiry, and knowledge—all of which are aimed at improving the quality of human living itself. Such critical problems as the disaffection of our youth, the deep-seated racism, and the millions subsisting in poverty that exist within the American society, when contrasted with such general achievements as our affluence, technology, and power as a nation point up that our principal emphasis has been on the educative process as a means, rather than as an end. The critical role which education as an institution must take in resolving those problems will be defaulted right from the outset unless the new priority balances the two key elements of the educative process in its conceptualization. In terms of the nation's need, the time has come not only to mandate education as a national priority but also to define this priority, so as to achieve the maximum benefits from the educative process for each citizen and thus for society as a whole.

Major institutional reforms in the public education system at all levels are imperative, if the concept of education as a basic human right is to be translated into a tangible reality for all of our citizens. To accomplish these reforms, a set of interlocking mechanisms must be developed that will bring about and then sustain needed changes in the operations of the three main components of the public education enterprise—governance, financing, and program. This set of mechanisms must accomplish the tasks of democratizing the governing structure of education at its various levels, of equalizing the financial support for education, and of redesigning programs that meet the identified needs of clients rather than the convenience of the system. Such mechanisms are essential if equal educational opportunity is ever going to be accorded to each American citizen as his basic right.

A quality education related to his identified needs must be guaranteed to every citizen. Education as a major public social institution must be made to function for people rather than against them, and the burdens of guaranteeing an equal educational opportunity to each citizen must reside with the nation itself. Thus, the legislative commitment must elevate the need for education to the status of a human right. And, in so doing, the poverty citizen—child, youth, or adult—is of especial concern. For it is this citizen, more than any other, who requires protection under the law.

AN EDUCATION BILL OF RIGHTS

In order to guarantee and to deliver to each person the right to an equal education, affirmative action must be taken by the Federal Congress. Formal guarantees—an education bill of rights—must be enacted which spell out clearly the substantive content of educational benefits that will be delivered to every American citizen. Constituting the first major element of the legislative proposal, educational rights are at the heart of the strategy and must include the following guarantees:

1. Recognizes the need of each person to receive educational services on a continuing basis, beginning with birth, which fulfill his personal requirements for full citizenship, economic productivity, and self-respect.

2. Assures that equality of educational opportunity be given its true meaning of equal preparation and readiness for all persons to function in all areas of society and in all economic pursuits on a

basis which does not discriminate among persons because of their racial, ethnic, or social status.

3. Assures that professional and employment opportunities are translated into specific forms of educational pursuit that permit an individual to decide upon and to achieve whichever profession or vocation is best for him according to his goals and capabilities.

4. Assures that technical and social obsolescence of employment opportunities is recognized through the continual revision of educational services to avert the training of persons for unavailable employment.

5. Requires that inequities in the distribution system be eliminated by a federal guarantee that resources will be available in terms of identifiable personal needs and in relation to reasonable state and local efforts toward providing those resources.

6. Requires that educational services be designed and implemented to meet the differing needs of individuals so as to afford their full expression and development.

7. Requires that educational services be designed to recognize and overcome the inequalities in environmental conditions in the home and neighborhood which inhibit effective school performance of poor children.

8. Requires that educational services be formulated in terms of objectives which recognize personal goals, as well as the goals of society.

9. Requires that, in the formulation of education policies and goals, full participation by the clients of the educational services be guaranteed so as to permit the creation of realistic and purposeful goals for the educational programs and services of the school.

10. Requires that vocational preparation and training for employment, as well as academic preparation, be guaranteed to all individuals who need this service and that the opportunities for such training must be related to the needs and employment opportunities of society at large.

These guarantees of educational rights are the key element to the national strategy for education being proposed here. They provide the principal substantive components for the development of the federal mandate, as well as the main points from which to derive a clear legislative definition of equal educational opportunity. However, before beginning their translation into specific terms for each of the elements that must be described in developing a proposal for major legislation, a brief look at the proposed rights in terms of securing necessary political support for enactment into law is necessary. A number of historical and legal precedents exist. The most obvious one is the Bill of Rights stated in the U. S. Constitution. A more recent precedent is to be found in the guarantees made to all citizens in the Civil Rights Act of 1964 and its amendments. Also, the Family Assistance Plan, proposed by the Nixon Administration for enactment into law, contains guarantees with regard to family income that elevate the need for a livable income to the status of being a human right.

In addition to precedent, the Education Bill of Rights recognizes the mounting pressures for social change as expressed through the rising expectations of minority and poverty groups, demands for improved educational programming by non-poor groups, and the need for a reaffirmation of an individual's rights in an increasingly depersonalized society. At the same time, the Education Bill of Rights, through its guarantees, implies that the public education system constitutes an institution that must be retained, but in an upgraded form and with a reformulated role that will benefit not just some citizens but all citizens. In effect, the essential aim of the Education Bill of Rights is to give reality to concepts, such as "equal opportunity," "universal free education," and "education to realize the full potential of each individual," which have been floating around American public education for years without any general implementation. Both in terms of precedent and need, the enactment of a set of educational guarantees as an essential element in the legislative proposal for the national strategy being advocated here is timely, urgent, and politically feasible.

Federal Funding Based on Individual Needs

The second key element in the legislative proposal for the national strategy for education is the way in which the federal funds must be conditioned in order to make the guarantees contained in the Education Bill of Rights a tangible reality for each citizen. These guarantees—reflecting such key concepts as education being a basic human right, the clear acceptance of a wide range of individual differences among citizens, and the provision of an equal educational opportunity to each citizen—must all be translated into a basic funding pattern that is sensitive to the guarantees in the allocation of federal resources.

As we have analyzed the experience with the programs of the opportunity strategy—and particularly ESEA Title I and its formula—for direction in designing a new funding formula to provide the financial basis for the guarantees proposed in the Education Bill of Rights, we have found four essential conditions which a new formula must address if it is to be effective in behalf of the clients and their education. Constituting the basis for deriving five criteria, these conditions are presented as the rationale for the formula.

RATIONALE

One of the conditions that must be met by the new funding formula is differential provision for the clients being served in terms of their varying needs. If there is anything that the experience with the education programs of the opportunity strategy has definitely demonstrated, it is that the living styles of the poor result in their having more basic unfulfilled human needs than do the living styles of the non-poor. Moreover, this experience has shown that the living styles of the poor impact upon the educative process in such a way as to seriously jeopardize the poverty individual's ability to perform effectively in a program that has been basically designed for non-poor individuals. Thus, to achieve an equal educational opportunity for the poverty individual, there must be adjustments made within the educational setting and its program that will take care of such needs. In monetary form, formula funding will, therefore, have to make provision for the special needs of the poor, above and beyond those of the non-poor, based on family income. An income criterion alone, however, will be insufficient.

Tied to this criterion, there must be another which identifies the needs of the clients and then computes the costs of the kinds of services which are required to provide the equal educational opportunity from a financial standpoint. Thus, the next criterion must be concerned with establishing cost guidelines for meeting the basic hierarchy of human needs—physical, social-emotional, and cognitive—essential to an individual's successful participation in the educative process.

A second condition that must be met by the new formula is recognizing the differences in the cost of providing effective educational programs to poor and non-poor clients at various stages in the educative process. The costs of effective programs vary from one educational level to another. Again, the knowledge gained from the programs and research of the opportunity strategy clearly demonstrates that educational programs should not only vary substantively for poverty clients, but that the programs should also begin at the earliest possible age for these clients in order to compensate for inadequacies in their environments, such as unfulfilled health and nutritional needs. However, the argument of one developmental level being necessarily more important than another must be discarded. If the poverty cycle is ever to be broken and the whole quality of life in our nation substantially improved—the twofold mission of this strategy—then all of the age levels from preschool through adult and continuing education must be viewed as having equal importance, although the actual dollar investments would presumably vary from level to level. Only by moving systematically at each age level according to the individual needs of the groups being served and by interlocking the efforts at one particular level with those of other levels can the education strategy being proposed hope to accomplish its mission. Hence, to the first and second criteria identified for inclusion in the formula, a third must be added—that of client age in relation to the educational developmental level.

The third condition that must be dealt with by the formula is the recognition of the differences in the availability of resources for public education at state and local levels. Quite apart from intrastate variations among local communities in the ability to pay for educational services, there are wide variations among the states in the amounts of dollar resources available to pay for effective educational services, as well as in the levels of effort being made to provide such services. The funding formula must, therefore, take into consideration the amounts of resources available for public education and the level of effort being made by each of the states in relation to the costs of effective educational programs for poor and non-poor citizens. Hence, a fourth criterion—geographic differences in state resources and levels of effort—is added to the requirements for the formula to be devised (intrastate differences among local communities are dealt with in chapter 9).

The last condition which the federal formula must address is the legal and practical side of dealing with the kinds of educational needs at the various levels proposed. At the elementary and secondary levels, there are compulsory school attendance requirements usually ranging from ages five or six to ages sixteen or seventeen. The result is that the state and local communities must provide educational programs at these levels and the clients must participate in them, if they cannot afford the expense of a non-public education. At the preschool and adult education levels, however, compulsory attendance is not required. Except for community and technical colleges available to high school graduates in some places, there is often little in the way of state or local resources that can be provided for preschool and adult education programs—critical as services at both these levels are to the adequate functioning of clients—and little in the way of choices available. Hence, a void has existed that the Federal Government has already begun to fill through such programs as Head Start, Job Corps, and Manpower Training.

At the higher education level, there is again no compulsory attendance requirement, although there is legal provision for public higher education services and funds for their support as a result of social need. When these services are coupled with those of private institutions, there is, for the first time in the educative process, a range of options open to a client depending upon his financial resources, his level of academic performance, and his geographical location. Theoretically, public higher education is available to all

qualified citizens; practically, the general outcome has been the
provision of services to those citizens who are typically economically favored. The Federal Government has already begun to fill
in the gaps at this level through providing financial assistance to
less favored citizens in the form of loans, grants, and work-study
programs. Hence, a fifth and somewhat different criterion emerges
for the federal formula that impacts upon the previously identified
criteria—that of adapting the formula through appropriate variations to the main legal and practical differences among the various
age-educational levels. These variations within the main formula
must, in accordance with the other criteria identified, reflect the
Federal Government's responsibility to assume an increasing share
of the costs at the various levels.

The five criteria derived from these four conditions must become
the bases of the federal formula if an equal educational opportunity is to be provided to the vast numbers of citizens to be
served from the fiscal standpoint. Also, this formula must be designed with distinct variations to accommodate the existing legal
and practical differences at the various age-educational levels.

FORMULA FOR FEDERAL FUNDING OF EDUCATION

When redefined into formula factors, the first four criteria, in
combination, must accomplish the basic task of differentiating the
poor from the non-poor clients at various age-educational levels in
their respective geographical locations according to both the costs
of effective educational programs and the level of state-local resources and effort. The fifth criterion, when translated into the
several formula variations, must accomplish the further task of
creating a fiscal ladder for the federal entitlements that reflect the
four basic formula factors. In order to accomplish the first task,
the first four criteria have been defined into the following formula
factors:

1. *Income Factor.*—The income factor for distinguishing (a)
poor from (b) non-poor clients makes use of the total personal family income as the basic index to determining client status. Remark-

ably accurate data can be produced by the U.S. Census Bureau on
the location of precise numbers of children—at any age level—in
census tracts that measure population in defined geographic areas
averaging 4,000 persons within each community. Using this dimension—and by frequent updating of the census—low-income poverty clients can be identified, located, and counted with great
precision. An additional aspect that must be taken into consideration is the large numbers of children per family in the low-income
bracket. Low-income families with more than four members
should be classified at a higher income level in the poverty income
threshold since the total personal income available must be divided
among additional persons. This numerical aspect reinforces the
need for a census-type poverty definition since it reflects both educational need and school burden—aspects which now depress the
quality of education in our poorer communities. The thresholds
should be based on assessments made by the Bureau of the Census
on an annual or biennial basis, so as to accommodate fluctuations
in the cost of living and dollar-purchasing power.

2. *Age Factor.*—Again, through the use of census data which
must be continually updated, the numbers of poor and non-poor
citizens that fall within the age-educational levels can be determined. Although the actual provision of funds would be based on
the number of individuals in programs, this factor would be able
to produce the potential entitlement all the way down to the individual school level if need be. The age-educational levels are
classified into (a) preschool, ages 1-5 for poor children and ages 4-5
for non-poor children; (b) elementary-middle grade, ages 6-13;
(c) secondary, ages 14-17; (d) higher education, ages 18-24; and (e)
adult and continuing education, ages 25-50.

3. *Human Needs Factor.*—The human needs factor assumes
that an average cost for the education-related services (e.g., health,
nutrition, counseling) and the educational services (e.g., reading,
mathematics) comprising an effective program, excluding construction costs, at each educational level can then be secured. The average program cost at each level is then obtained by pricing out
effective programs, identified by means of performance criteria, in
terms of the overall cost of each of the programs included on a per

capita basis. From these costs, a national average cost for a total quality program at that particular educational level is then computed. In making this cost analysis at each of the levels, programs serving both the poor and non-poor must be balanced. The result obtained from applying this factor is a national average cost for an effective program on a per capita basis at each educational level, which then serves as the baseline for determining the varying amounts of federal entitlement that would be needed for a given set of poor and non-poor clients at any level. The human needs factor is also important to the geographic factor which follows.

4. *Geographic Resource Factor.*—The geographic resource factor has five aspects: (a) the average per capita income of each state; (b) the national average per capita income of the United States as a whole; (c) the percentage of its total income being expended by each state on education; (d) the percentage of the total national income for the United States being expended on education; and (e) the state average expenditure per student for education.

The four factors provide the necessary fiscal framework for accomplishing the equal educational opportunity for poor and non-poor clients at the federal level. The conversion of these factors into the formula variations that differentiate the entitlements for these clients, according to income level, educational needs, age, and location, is presented, beginning with the elementary–middle grade and secondary variation.

Termed here as the compulsory formula variation because of the school attendance requirement, the federal entitlements within the two age-educational levels included would be derived in the following steps:

a. The national average cost of an effective education program on a per capita basis is computed for each educational level, excluding construction costs. From the groups of programs analyzed at these levels, per capita program costs to be used as the national averages will result (Factors 2 and 3).

b. The national average per capita taxable income of the United States is determined (Factor 4-b).

c. The average per capita available taxable income is determined on a state-by-state basis (Factor 4-a).

d. Using the national average per capita income of the United States (Factor 4-b), the percentage by which any state is either above or below this national average income in terms of its average per capita income (Factor 4-a) is determined.

e. Through this percentage determination, the specific differences among the states provide the basis for states below the national average per capita income (Factor 4-b) to become eligible for a special override in their entitlements.

f. For a state with a percentage that is below the national average in terms of its average per capita income, the average program costs at each of the educational levels (Factor 3) are increased by that percentage by which the state is below the national average per capita income, provided that the state is devoting at least the national average of its resources to public education (Factors 4-c and 4-d). All other states would only be eligible for the national average program cost.

g. The differences between each state's average per pupil expenditure for education (Factor 4-e) after equalization (described in chapter 9 as the financial equity tactic) and the costs of the average quality programs (adjusted for override for those states which qualify in step f) are then computed for each particular educational level. The figures comprising the differences for a particular state become the basis for determining the federal entitlement to that state at each of the educational levels on a per capita basis.

h. In order to determine the actual amount to which a state would be entitled, two multipliers are used based on the number of poor (Factor 1-a) and non-poor clients (Factor 1-b) at each educational level within a particular state. In the case of poor clients, the multiplier consists of the amount computed in step g above (the differences between the average state expenditure for public education and the cost of the quality programs at each level) by 100 per cent of the total number of poor clients at each level. For non-poor clients, the multiplier is again this amount but by 50 per cent of the total number of non-poor clients at each level. Federal entitlements should not in any event exceed 100 per cent of the state average expenditure per pupil (Factor 4-e) for non-poor children and 200 per cent for poor children.

Although the general manner in which the compulsory formula variation would produce differentiated entitlements at the two age-educational levels has been described, an example of this variation in operation serves as a clarification here. It shows the compulsory formula variation applied to a deep south state that is eligible for special assistance in comparison with a far west state that is above the average income for the United States. While most of the figures used here are derived from the latest statistics available at the time of this writing, the figure used for the national average cost of program is a "best judgment" estimate. Only one national average program cost is estimated for the example shown in Table 1.

Two age levels are also included within the second formula variation—preschool and adult-continuing education. It is labeled as permissive because of the lack of compulsory attendance requirements, the general gaps in the availability of such services, and the choice of whether to participate or not which the individual—or his representative in the case of a young child—must make. Employing generally the same factors and constraints as noted in the compulsory variation, the permissive formula variation would operate in the following manner:

1. Because of the void in existing services, combined with their high need and low capability, the states in the special override category (step f) would receive a federal entitlement computed at 90 per cent of the national average program cost on a per capita basis for the preschool and the adult-continuing education levels. And the state-local contribution would be 10 per cent of the cost. In the case of preschool program, poor children would become eligible, subject to the availability of programs (point 3 below), beginning at age one, while non-poor children would become eligible, beginning at age 4.

2. All other states would be eligible for a federal entitlement

TABLE 1

Estimated Per Capita Entitlements for Two States
Using Proposed Compulsory Formula Variation for
Federal Funding of Education*

FACTORS		STATE A—eligible for special assistance in federal override	STATE B— eligible for regular federal entitlement
FI-a.	Entitlement per client (poor)	$868	$278
F1-b.	Entitlement per client (non-poor)	$434	$139
F2, 3.	Average program cost per educational level	Elementary @ $1200	Elementary @ $1200
F4-a.	State per capita income	$2,780	$4,272
F4-b.	National per capita income	$3,680	$3,680
F4-c.	State effort	5.83%	6.40%
F4-d.	National effort	5.46%	5.46%
F4-e.	State average per pupil expenditure	$620	$922

* Source of baseline figures is DHEW/USOE, *Digest of Educational Statistics, 1970,* Tables 75 and 76, pp. 51–58. F4-e excludes capital outlay and interest on school debt; the figures represent estimated operating expenditures for 1969–70 school year on a per capita basis using average daily attendance.

of 80 per cent of the national average program cost, and would be required to contribute 20 per cent of this cost from their own resources. The 80:20 proportion proposed for these states is based on the assumption that while a gap exists, such states do have some capability at these levels and that there is a high need level in these states as well. The same age constraints would apply to the provision of services to poor and non-poor children at the preschool level as those programs became available.

3. In recognition of the need for adequate time in which to

plan for and to train personnel to implement preschool programs
on the scale envisioned here, it is proposed that such programs
should be phased in a year at a time, beginning, for example, with
all four- or five-year olds.

4. Two contingencies are proposed in order for funds to be
provided according to the entitlements. First, to insure the inclusion of poor clients in preschool programs, no funds would be
made available for these programs unless the number of poor children being served in relation to non-poor children is within 5 per
cent of that state's percentage of poor children at the particular
age level(s) involved, according to the latest updating of the census data. Second, to insure that maximum benefits would accrue to
both poor and non-poor children through preschool education as a
preventive measure against the accumulation of learning problems, no funds would be made available at the elementary-middle
grade and secondary levels to a particular state unless it is engaging in a state-wide preschool program effort.

5. While state participation in preschool programs is proposed as a mandatory requirement for the state to receive federal
funds for the elementary-middle grade and secondary levels, no
such requirement is proposed for programs at the adult-continuing
education level. State participation at this level would be achieved
through the financial incentive of the federal grant combined with
a guarantee of full opportunity for universal client participation.

One age-educational level—higher education—is included
within the third formula variation. It is termed as optional because
of the availability of services at this level; these services tend to be
more available to some than to others; and the individual choices
involved in whether or not to participate—and, if so, where to participate. Employing some of the same factors but with a refine-
ment for Factor 1, Income, the optional formula variations for
higher education would work in the following way:

1. The various types of federal entitlements would be based
on family income divided into population quartiles. Entitlements
would be related to national estimated costs of higher education

to students attending various classes of schools. Grant entitlements for students would represent direct cash based on their income quartiles; work-study payments would represent funds earned by students on jobs established for them (usually at the institution they attend); loans would represent amounts borrowed by students under government-insured loan provisions; and personal resources would be amounts which students should provide from their own sources. Table 2 shows the proposed percentage levels of entitlement, beginning with Quartile 1 representing the lowest population income level, for which a client at the undergraduate level would be eligible. The percentages show the maximum benefits for which a client in a particular quartile could apply.

TABLE 2

Proposed Per Capita Federal Entitlements by Per Cent
for Higher Education Based on Income Quartiles

INCOME QUARTILE	GRANT	WORK-STUDY AND LOAN	PERSONAL RESOURCES
1 (low)	50	40	10
2	25	50	25
3	—	50	50
4	—	25	75

2. Upon a client showing proof of both admission to a higher education institution and income level, a voucher would be issued to the institution on behalf of the student in the amount of the combined assistance to which he is entitled. Payment is then made to the institution for the student for that period of time in which he is enrolled as an undergraduate student.

3. Recognition that an institution does not support its programs on tuition and fees alone and that students from low-income backgrounds often have special educational and education-related needs, an institution would receive for every student grant a corresponding grant in the same amount to cover excess institutional costs. Both the undergraduate and the institutional grants would be awarded on an annual basis.

4. For an institution offering advanced study (beyond the baccalaureate level), a grant award based on 5 per cent of the total number of clients within the baccalaureate group and the national average program cost would be made to the institution. This grant award would be used by the institution to offer special assistance to clients for graduate study, provided that the particular institution allocates not less than 50 per cent of this amount to clients with incomes classified in the first and second quartiles.

For all age levels and eligible citizens, it is estimated that the combined federal entitlement would be somewhere in the vicinity of $40 billion in its first full year of operation, and that approximately five years would be required before full operation could be achieved. The amount cited here would subsume the current federal education program expenditures; that is, the new formula with its variations would either replace or absorb all currently existing formula and granting authority. It should be pointed out that this figure is acceptable when compared with the cost of maintaining some 25 million people on welfare with little guarantee that the poverty cycle will ever be broken in a major way. Over time, the investment approach to human resources through education is likely to be less costly—both in economic and in human terms—than the maintenance approach of keeping large numbers of people treading water on a generation-to-generation basis through welfare. Such comparisons put the amount of the entitlement under the proposed federal formula into a budgetary/ fiscal perspective which is definitely feasible, but they do not directly address the extent to which the formula with its several variations is likely to be politically feasible as well. A brief analysis of the formula in terms of its potential for political acceptance serves as the concluding portion of this chapter.

In general, the formula recognizes that education is an urgent human need and that, by and large, an overall improvement in the quality of education is an urgent need as well. The formula provides for both needs to be met through (a) utilizing general program standards at each age-educational level, (b) making the funds available to provide local programs adapted to the needs of the clients in line with these standards, and (c) taking into consideration the differential costs of educating our citizens according to their needs and their particular developmental stages in the educational process. In providing for education as a general need as well as for education in an upgraded form for all citizens, the formula is headed in the direction of providing the equal educational opportunity that is at the heart of educational accountability.

The formula realistically focuses on the fact that the fifty states are not of equal strength in their resource capability for educational services. An adjustment for this inequality provides special assistance to those states which are more limited than others in terms of resource capability and which are also making a more than average effort in the area of their educational expenditures. Through such assistance, the formula would favor states with large proportions in their populations of poor clients, and provide additional monies for the kinds of educational programs that are needed for both poor and non-poor clients. In providing special assistance as a part of the entitlement to some states and regular entitlements to all other states, the formula addresses the need for equalization of resources provided from the federal level, in return for internal equalization of financial resources within each state. As is politically necessary for the legislative enactment of education formulas, it is to be noted that this formula would work to the advantage of the southern states.

In this connection, the formula directly takes into consideration the fact that the provision of an equal educational opportunity through full-service programs to the poor clients is more costly than its provision for non-poor clients. Recognizing that this increased cost is a matter of acting in the best interest of the general welfare of the nation, the Federal Government should—indeed, must—put up the money for the extra costs involved, a task already begun by the educational and education-related programs of the opportunity strategy. With the rising costs of and demands for education at all levels, coupled with the rising costs of and demands for other public services, the states and their local communities—even after internal equalization—will be unable to carry the extra costs entailed in educating the poor clients.

The formula assumes that the Federal Government has a special responsibility for filling in the gaps that now exist at every educational level, and especially those in preschool and adult education. Already engaged in the gap-filling process through a wide variety of categorical aid programs, the Federal Government must now move to complete this process in a systematic and sound way. For example, the formulas for the Nixon Administration's day-care program and higher education legislation can be viewed as major components in the strategy being proposed here. The new multi-level formula, as stated, offers a clear and comprehensive alternative to the categorical aid hodgepodge that has grown up over the years. And, as an alternative, the formula is particularly timely since most public and non-public school systems and institutions of higher education are becoming caught in the tightening vise of financial precariousness and increasing client demands. Despite the likely hue and cry from the professional lobbies that the formula with its variations is tantamount to federal control of education, the fact of the matter is that education, in general, is facing a combined financial and programmatic crisis. It is this fact—and particularly its financial aspect—that may make the outcry more *pro forma* than substantive. It seems reasonable to anticipate that the education lobbies, because of the potential magnitude of the money involved, may very well accept a trade-off of federal guidelines and an active federal role in return for the rescue funds. And the hard-pressed state and city governments may also find the trade-off a fair exchange. Client advocate groups, such as the NAACP, NWRO, and Common Cause, are apt to support the formula with its funding variations if they are convinced that it will work to make the system accountable to their clients and the equal educational opportunity a reality. Their opposition is assured, however, if the formula is perceived as thinly disguised general aid under the full control of the education establishment. If the clients and their lobbies were notably absent at the birth of ESEA in 1965—and Title I in particular—they are likely to be very much present for the legislative process on a proposal of the magnitude of the one being advocated here in the 1970's.

Thus, the formula, as a translation of the Education Bill of

Rights, is aimed at achieving, from a fiscal standpoint, the equal educational opportunity and its corollary—institutional accountability—now so urgently needed. For this reason, it should be incorporated into the legislative mandate as its second major element, the first being the Education Bill of Rights. However, these elements alone will not be sufficient for the legislative mandate. One other element should also be incorporated into this mandate—the educational program in terms of its main dimensions.

9

The Educational
Program Tactics

LIKE THE FORMULA, the educational program is a translation of the Education Bill of Rights, and is proposed as the third major element for inclusion in the legislative mandate. Accordingly, the several tactics making up the educational program are all aimed at achieving the goal of an equal educational opportunity through providing a framework for creating genuine client-centered educational programs and institutional accountability. In actuality, at the post-secondary level, this framework is already provided through the specific formula variations. That is, education at the post-secondary level is a matter of personal choice and presumably the individual making this choice has the maturity to do so. Moreover, except for the functionally illiterate, he has several options available to him for furthering his education. To explain further, the formula variations constitute a de facto voucher system for clients at the post-secondary level which would make personal choices among existing options and the client demands for new options a practical matter. Combining the voucher system that would be created through the client entitlements under the formula with client demands and their maturity creates a tactic at the post-secondary level that should exert enough leverage to result in the provision of equal educational opportunity and institutional accountability.

However, the combination of formula, options, and client characteristics that produces a workable tactic at the higher education and adult-continuing education levels is not repeated at the other three developmental levels. Special tactics are needed at the pre-school, elementary-middle grade, and secondary levels because of the general lack of options for most clients at these levels, the immaturity of the clients, the compulsory attendance requirements for all but the preschool level, the huge number of clients to be served, and the currently unstated premises of the system (chapter 7), which serve as roadblocks to the goal of equal educational opportunity. For these reasons, the tactics presented here as the educational program are specifically designed for the first three developmental levels and are proposed for the critical areas of educational programming—intrastate financing, performance standards, and the decision-making structure.

As a preliminary to the presentation of the new tactics, a definition of the term "tactic" is given. As used here, a tactic is a set of devices or techniques employed to carry out a specific segment of the strategy, which is the master design. Defined in this manner, a tactic has breadth in its coverage and substantive and procedural aspects as well. With this definition in mind, we begin with a description of the proposed tactic in the financing area. The likelihood of gaining political acceptance for this and the other tactics is considered after all three have been described.

Financial Equity Tactic

The financial equity tactic proposes that the federal monies provided by the formula (chapter 8) be made available on a contingency funding basis as an essential first step to delivering on a genuinely client-centered education. It is also proposed that to achieve this equitable distribution of fiscal resources, there must be a major reform of the existing financial arrangements within the states themselves. Three basic procedures are presented through which to accomplish this reform.

EQUITABLE APPORTIONMENT OF STATE AND LOCAL RESOURCES

As a precondition to qualifying for federal funds under the proposed formula, each state must be required to equalize its state and local funds for all of its clients. Our proposal in this regard

follows that made by Coons, Cline, and Sugarman in their exhaus-
tive study of state educational financing. Their major proposition
is that "the quality of public education may not be a function of
wealth other than the wealth of the state as a whole."[1] And we
further endorse the major procedures they delineate for translating this proposition into action. These procedures are, as
follows:

1. The state should take over the financing of public education.
2. The state should secure from all school districts those
sums of money, including property taxes, and then redistribute
these monies on an equal apportionment basis computed on the
number of clients to be served.[2]

While some additional factors might presumably have to be
taken into consideration at the state level, such as the cost of educational services in a large city as compared with the cost of such
services in small towns, the basic procedures would be mandatory
for a state to be eligible for the federal funds. With these procedures in effect, the present set of inequities which now exist at
the state and local levels would be overcome. Also, a floor would
be established that would guarantee each client an equal portion
of the state's available resources for educational services. This floor
would constitute the first critical step to an equal educational
opportunity from the financial standpoint at both the state and
local levels.

After the state has equalized its financial resources in terms of
all of its educational clients, the federal funds, through the proposed formula, can then be used to supplement the state-local
contributions, where the client needs for an equal educational
opportunity are the greatest. Moreover, the proportion of a state's
financial resources going into the per capita contribution for education can be used as an indicator of both the priority which a
particular state is placing on education and the level of effort
which it is making. In turn, this indicator can become a criterion
for awarding additional federal monies on an incentive basis.

The requirement for state equalization of its funds as a precondition to receiving federal funds is one general procedure of the financial equity tactic. Another procedure is concerned with a new role for the clients themselves.

THE CLIENT AS LEGAL BENEFICIARY OF THE FEDERAL FUNDS

If an equal educational opportunity is to be delivered on through a client-centered education, the client himself (or his surrogate in the case of a young child) must have a major role in determining how and for what he will be educated. In order to guarantee that he will have this role, we propose that the client shall become the legal beneficiary of the federal funds, since he has legal rights to an education that must provide him with an equal educational opportunity—and, thus, an education that is sufficient for his needs. As legal beneficiary of these funds, we further propose that the client (or his surrogate) would be the only person who would be able to certify the use by a particular school district of the funds that have been paid by the Federal Government on his behalf.

In other words, the clients, singly or in groups, would be entering into a contractual relationship with a particular educational agency for a specified time period, such as an academic year, in which they and the agency would agree upon what educational and education-related services would be needed for the clients to receive an equal educational opportunity. Unless the clients sign the contract releasing the funds to the agency for the services agreed to, subject to a test of reasonableness to avoid excessive demands, the federal funds cannot be used by that or any other agency. The federal funds would be held in trust by the state pending proof of client certification, which would be transmitted to it by the local educational agency involved. The amount for which particular clients would be eligible would be determined by the formula factors and by the level of state-local effort. At the end of the specified time period, the clients would then certify whether or not the specific services described in the contract had, indeed, been delivered. If such services were not delivered, the educational agency would then face the denial of the funds available to these clients in the future, as well as possible legal action.

Through both the initial certification (signing the contract for a specified set of services) and the follow-up certification after the particular time period involved (affirming whether or not such services were provided), the clients can exert a powerful influence on achieving the kind of education that is specifically tailored for them. In the case of poor clients, this certification procedure would have particularly potent leverage on a particular educational agency, because their federal entitlement would represent a large supplement to the state-local contribution being paid in their behalf. A precedent for this procedure now exists in—of all places—the program of assistance to schools in federally affected areas (impact aid), where children are identified for assistance on the basis of parental employment or residence on federal property. In this instance, the parent is requested to submit a questionnaire which gives relevant employment and residential data, on the basis of which the local school receives a federal payment on behalf of each "federally connected" child. We propose to go only a step further by requiring parental certification over the use of federal funds as well as over its receipt by the local educational system.

One further general procedure remains to be described for the financial equity tactic. This procedure is concerned with the utilization of the proposed federal formula (presented in chapter 8).

UTILIZATION OF THE FEDERAL FORMULA

The proposed federal formula is not to be construed as providing automatic funding for educational programs to the states and their local educational agencies. Rather, from the fiscal standpoint alone, the sums of money that would become available to the states and their agencies would be subject to two contingencies. First, the reform of state educational financing patterns should be carried out, so that a uniform base or floor is established on a per capita basis for educational expenditure. Second, the client certification of the federal funds must be carried out since the client would, in fact, be the legal grantee, while the state would be the trustee of such funds and the local agency the administrator.

With these contingencies being applied, the formula also goes further in delivering on education as a basic human right. On the one hand, it recognizes equal educational opportunity as the heart of this right by making specific fiscal adjustments for different economic groups at different age levels. These adjustments are essential if the programs to be offered are to meet the needs of the clients being served. On the other hand, through the sheer magnitude of its monetary contribution coupled with its contingencies, the proposed formula provides a potent mechanism for gaining the kind of leverage on the educational system that will be required, if client-centered education is ever to become a reality for the millions of clients to be served.

In describing the formula and its use, the procedures or subtactics comprising the financial equity tactic are completed. However, a financial tactic alone is insufficient for the educational program change that is needed; a substantive program performance tactic is required as well.

Education Performance Tactic

If the financial equity tactic is designed to deliver on education as a human right from the fiscal standpoint, the proposed educational performance tactic is designed to deliver on it from the standpoint of the educative process to be engaged in by the client. In order to achieve this right, the educational performance tactic —like the financial equity one—must possess procedures which produce substantive changes in the relationships between the client and the school and in the kinds and quality of the education-related and educational services offered to him. Three procedures are proposed which are imperative to achieving genuinely client-centered education.

PERFORMANCE STANDARDS

The first procedure consists of the use of clearly defined educational performance standards, which should be stated in their
generalized form as broad program guidelines for client-centered
education at every level and which should also constitute the
basis for developing subsequent contractual relationships concerning the provision of these programs for the clients. Stated as an
integral part of the legislative mandate, these performance standards should have the following characteristics. First, they should
be directly derived from the Bill of Education Rights. Second,
they should be stated in such a way that the main burden for the
success of the educational program is placed not on the client
but on the educational system itself. That is, the mandate should
clearly state the general standards being established in a form
which clearly reverses the practice of fitting clients to program
needs and of punishing clients for program failures. Third, these
standards should be formulated in such a way as to afford the
bases for the design and implementation of programs at various
age-educational levels according to differing client needs and
abilities and for subsequent evaluations of the extent to which
the programs are successful in terms of meeting these client needs
at various levels. Fourth, they should reflect an expanded and
humanized concept of the educative process in the American
society. That is, these standards must encompass more than the
external success criterion of economic-social status and the internal success criterion of academic achievement, such as reading.
Criteria, such as educating our citizens to become constructive
change agents within their personal and professional lives and
educating our citizens for rational self-mastery through genuine
self-understanding, must also be reflected in these standards.

Having been stated as broad program guidelines within the
legislative mandate, the standards can then be used as the legal
basis for developing sets of contractual relationships to guarantee
that the clients are actually receiving an equal educational opportunity through client-centered programs. As a precondition to
making certain that such programs will be provided to the clients,

the legislative mandate should stipulate that educational agencies and institutions will be required (a) to guarantee that they will design their programs in accordance with the general performance standards as stated, and (b) to agree to having both their formal applications and resulting program operations evaluated in terms of these standards. Securing these guarantees must become the essential next step required of the states, local school systems, and other educational entities in order to receive the federal monies under the formula entitlement for the clients being served. Without these guarantees formulated in a contractual relationship, the goal of revitalizing and humanizing education for the clients will be jeopardized from the outset. This contractual relationship in various forms is projected to extend through the several educational governance levels to the clients themselves. This relationship is again mentioned here, because it is derived from the standards and is involved in the other procedures for this tactic.

However, neither the standards nor their incorporation into contracts describe the specific ways and means for assisting both the clients and the educational agencies and institutions in developing operating programs derived from the standards. These ways and means are another task with which the proposed legislative mandate must be concerned.

PERFORMANCE LEARNING DESIGNS

As the second procedure of the performance tactic, the new legislative mandate should stipulate that educational agencies or institutions at both state and local levels will be required to develop fully detailed educational plans or learning designs in accordance with identified client needs and the national average program costs at whatever age-educational levels are to be served. As conceived here, the learning design is the blueprint, first, for identifying and organizing the elements of the educative process into a promising delivery system for the client-centered education in accordance with the general standards, and second, for assessing the effectiveness of the resultant programs in making client-centered education a tangible reality. In other words, at both state and local levels, the learning design is a procedure for knowing what resources are required to meet the general standards, for arranging these resources into unified programs for the clients, for establishing clear bases on which to make continual improvements in the programs, and for establishing their substance.

In addition to requiring learning designs, the legislative mandate should specify the critical components that must be included in all designs to be considered for funding through the formula. While subsequent administrative regulations and guidelines would develop the major characteristics of these elements in some detail, this requirement is necessary to assure that the process of educational program renewal will be set into motion and is principally based on the experience with the programs of the opportunity strategy—and, specifically, with ESEA Title I.

Four components are deemed essential. The first consists of the client needs in relation to the general performance standards. This assessment must address both a finding of the characteristics of the client, in terms of a well-defined hierarchy of needs, and a determination of how those needs will impact on the client's general potential for learning. For the clients, the assessment of their needs will become a tangible first step on the pathway to client-centered education. The second component consists of the specific performance criteria or objectives that all aspects and daily activities of the operating program will be designed to achieve. Derived from the general standards as stated in the enabling legislation, the specific performance criteria must reflect the characteristics of those standards adapted for the particular clients and age-educational levels involved. In addition to providing the bases for developing, implementing, and evaluating the programs, these criteria should be interrelated from level to level. The third component consists of the full description of the program activities for both the instructional and supportive services aspects. The fourth component is the staff development plan, which, in particular, should provide for the continued improvement of the instructional and supportive services staff, since they constitute the key translation point for the entire strategy.

Thus, the learning design is the mechanism through which a

tangible form of the client-centered education can actually be tailored for, certified by, and delivered to a specific group of clients. It should be viewed as the starting point for delivering on the equal educational opportunity—and, therefore, subject to change and modification as experience with the design in action accumulates. Viewed in this manner, the design provides a rational basis for making changes to improve the ongoing local programs as well as the state-wide design in terms of the clients. And it is with these changes in mind that one further procedure of this tactic is proposed that deals with responsibility for and accountability in the educative process.

PERFORMANCE REPORTS TO THE PUBLIC

As a part of the responsibility associated with a public trust, both the state and local educational agencies and institutions should be required by the legislation to make periodic reports on their educational performances. The state and local agencies and institutions should also be required to utilize knowledgeable persons, not in their direct employ, to study the extent to which the programs being offered do, indeed, meet the needs of the clients being served.

The reports of a local agency or institution should be made widely available for public reaction and comment. Moreover, a feedback system should be developed at the local level that permits the agency or institution to respond constructively and responsibly to reactions from its various constituencies. Then, the local units should transmit these reports, as a part of their contract, with accompanying constituency reactions to the state for analysis and compilation into a state-wide report to the Federal Government. Finally, addressing many of the same program areas but with a broadened scope, the state report should also include a section which provides evidence concerning the type and quality of leadership and technical assistance that it has given to the local agencies and institutions.

Through state and local reports containing full accounts of the education being offered in all its various aspects and through encouraging responses from both the participating clients and the general public, the education program can add another procedure that is directed toward accountability on behalf of its clients and the effective discharging of a public trust. Operating in this manner, the educational performance tactic, combined with the financial equity tactic, provides mechanisms for the client-centered program and the fair distribution of state-local resources that can reach all the way to the client in his classroom. One other tactic, which serves as the linchpin for the legislative mandate, is concerned with educational governance or the decision-making process.

Decision-making Tactic

The decision-making tactic of the new education strategy must be potent enough to guarantee to the client his basic right as a citizen to have adequate control over his educational destiny, if he is ever to receive an education that is specifically designed for him. At the same time, this tactic must have a liberating influence upon the system itself so that teachers and other staff will be freed to work creatively with their clients, rather than to have their ideas and firsthand knowledge of client needs stifled by a predetermined program that serves the needs of the system. The power over educational decision-making must be redistributed through the creation of new and effective mechanisms or procedures, if equal educational opportunity is ever to have reality as a basic human right.

With the enabling legislation in mind, four procedures are proposed for the decision-making tactic. One of these—already introduced in the financial equity tactic—is the performance guarantee or contract at the various levels of education. Described for the first time in this section are three other procedures: the client school board, an appeals system which involves a new concept of social accountability, and a set of alternative decision patterns over funding, all designed to serve, rather than to penalize, the clients in case of deficient system performance at either the local or state levels. The four procedures are described as they are variously translated at the several governance levels in education.

DECISION-MAKING PROCEDURES AT THE LOCAL LEVEL

At the heart of the decision-making tactic at all levels lies the procedure of the performance contract. At the local level, the contracts would be signed by specific clients or their representatives with whatever local agency or institution is to provide them with the educational and education-related services that they need to receive an equal educational opportunity. Only when both parties (clients or their representatives and the agency) have agreed in writing upon the specifications for the educational program to be provided would the federal contribution to the clients' education be released to the institution to be used in their behalf.

In addition, there must be a procedure whereby the clients can organize themselves in order to maintain an adequate control over the program during the particular time period of their contracts. This need for ongoing control brings up the second procedure, the community client board, which should be created as an extension of the typical school board. Conceived as operating at the neighborhood community level, this board should, after the per capita availability of all financial resources has been determined, have full decision-making authority in the areas of personnel, program, and finance. Moreover, this board should have the authority to initiate fiscal and/or educational program reviews in instances where there is documented evidence of institutional failure or unwillingness to deliver on the specifications of the contracts at a reasonable level. The board should have access to such legal services as may be needed to enforce the terms and conditions of the contracts. This kind of authority is necessary if the clients are to maintain genuine control over their educational destiny. Finally, the client boards should be required to have a membership composition that proportionally reflects the clients being served.

Two areas of decision-making—program review and access to legal procedure—make up the appeal mechanism, which is essential to guarantee to the clients an adequate control over the program while it is in progress. As one part of this mechanism, the program review is proposed as a device whereby a local client board, by filing simultaneous appeals with the state and federal levels, can ask for assistance in correcting deficiencies in programs being provided by an educational agency through the use of an impartial and qualified review team. These appeals, with accompanying documentation, would be filed only after a reasonable time period had been given for the agency in question to correct the specified deficiencies. Should an adequate state-level review fail to be conducted within a reasonable period of time after the local appeal with its documentation is adjudged to be valid, then a review initiated from the federal level would become mandatory.

If the appeal process, using the program-review device, fails to produce the necessary corrective action within the time periods specified, or if the client board has no confidence in this device based on past experience, the board should have the prerogative to take direct legal action. In combination, the Education Bill of Rights, the performance contract, and adequate documentation of the deficient performance of the particular agency involved—including past experience—provide a legitimate legal basis for court action. However, more than a deficient performance of an institution based on a contract is at issue here. Since it is the individual clients who have been and will continue to be the ones to suffer the most from inadequate institutional performances throughout their entire lives, the real issue with regard to legal action must be viewed as that of educational malpractice. As defined here, educational malpractice is based on the humanistic concept that an inadequate performance of a major social institution, such as the schools, can create permanent damage to the personal, social, and economic lifetime expectancies of an individual. At the present time, the concept of educational malpractice, from the legal standpoint, is founded on the equal protection clause of the Fourteenth Amendment to the Constitution, which also provides the clearest rationale for the proposed Education Bill of Rights. That amendment guarantees to each individual equal protection under the law; and, therefore, the denial of an equal education and the opportunity for that education is subject to legal redress of grievances.

As is evident in the three procedures specifically proposed for the decision-making tactic at the local level, the intent is clearly to place the educational institution in the position of being accountable where it counts the most—to its clients at the local level. To accomplish this educational accountability, the power over the utilization of available resources must be redistributed at this level, so as to make certain that the clients themselves have a major voice in determining why, how, and for what they will be educated. To insure that the clients have this voice, the decision-making procedures at the state level must also deliberately reinforce the new procedures proposed for the local level.

DECISION-MAKING PROCEDURES AT THE STATE LEVEL

At the state level, the procedures generally parallel those proposed for the local level, but on a broadened scale. That is, performance contracts are negotiated between a state educational agency and the eligible local agencies in compliance with the state's contract with the Federal Government. In order to strengthen the role of the state in achieving educational accountability on behalf of the clients, the state must (a) certify the existence of signed client contracts and local client-board approval as verification of the legitimacy of and the need for the local agency's criteria, (b) review and approve the budget plan for the specified time period of the contracts for reasonableness vis-à-vis existing financial resources and client needs, and (c) secure an agreement from each local agency for the state to conduct a full fiscal audit of the execution of the contracts in terms of the federal and state-local contributions. These conditions must be met by local agencies before the state can release any federal funds to them. In the event that a local agency refuses to meet any one of these conditions, the state shall either withhold federal funds until all of them are satisfactorily met or negotiate, with the help of the local client board, with another agency.

As at the local level, there is the same need at the state level to insure that the clients will have some direct control over decision-making. Therefore, a state-wide client board should be created which supersedes any such boards currently in existence. Moreover, this board should have a membership composition which proportionally reflects the kinds of clients being served. It should have the same general decision-making authority at the state level as that proposed for the local-level client boards, with several proposed additions. They consist of (a) redefining school district boundaries, (b) monitoring federal and state-local resource allocation, (c) monitoring the performance of the state educational agency, (d) stipulating changes in state-level personnel and program in conjunction with the terms and conditions of the state's contracts with either the Federal Government or the local agencies, and (e) appointing the state superintendent.

Through the procedures proposed for the state level, the development of educational accountability on behalf of the clients is continued. On the one hand, the state can now require and receive this accountability on behalf of the clients from its local agencies. And, on the other, the state educational agency itself can become an accountable institution with regard to all of the clients. Concerned with completing the development of this accountability at all levels, the federal procedures follow.

DECISION-MAKING PROCEDURES AT THE FEDERAL LEVEL

At the federal level, the previously described procedures at the other levels are reflected and a new procedure is introduced. Again, there is the performance contract which the states and the Federal Government would sign. Upon signing its contract, the state becomes the duly authorized legal agent of the Federal Government for carrying out the terms and conditions of that contract for the time period specified on behalf of the clients. Included in each federal-state contract should be the performance criteria or standards which have been developed by the state. With regard to the federal-state performance contract, the federal governance level should have full authority to (a) negotiate and approve contracts with the states, (b) allocate federal resources based on these contracts when a particular contract meets the necessary requirements, (c) monitor the state educational agency performance for compliance with the terms and conditions of the contract, (d) conduct program reviews resulting from complaints and appeals, and (e) implement alternative patterns of providing funds for the clients in local programs in the event of documented proof of state or local lack of compliance with any or all of the terms and conditions of the agreed-upon contracts.

The appeal mechanism would basically be concerned with complaints and appeals that emerge via the administrative route of the educational governance levels rather than as a result of court action. For court action, the decision would be binding, although subject to change pending a reversal by a higher court. With the administrative route, the appeals would receive an investigation on site by one or more qualified review teams for the purpose of determining whether or not corrective action was required. Based on its study, the recommendations of the review team(s) would become binding upon the federal level in terms of its response to the situation, including a recommendation that would require the implementation of an alternative pattern of funding, which could exclude the state and/or the local agency from any handling of or benefits from the federal funds. These review teams would, in effect, parallel the client boards at the other educational levels.

Already alluded to is the proposed new procedure at the federal level which consists of a mechanism for alternative funding patterns. Based on the extent to which the educational performances of institutions at the state and local levels do meet acceptability as specified by the contracts, the intent of the mechanism is to guarantee to each client the continued federal contribution to his education to which he is entitled under the Education Bill of Rights and the formula. Like the mechanisms comprising the other procedures, this mechanism is also concerned with providing the clients with control over their educational destiny.

Under the primary pattern of the mechanism, the Federal Government would, as a result of its performance contract with a state, provide funds to the state for transmittal to the clients at the local level, and the state would receive an accompanying amount

for administrative handling. In turn, the state, based on its contract with the Federal Government and its contracts with the local
educational agencies—the latter being certified by the community
client boards—would allocate the specified amounts of the federal
contribution due to each client through the local educational
agency involved. When the monies arrived at the local level, they
would be used for the educational and education-related services
agreed upon in the client-institution contracts and fully described
in the performance learning design. Thus, the typical and primary
funding pattern would be federal to state to the local clients via
the local educational agency or institution. In this way, the primary pattern underscores the principle that the control over educational decision-making should reside where the educative
process is taking place—at the local level. As long as all educational governance levels perform in accordance with the Education Bill of Rights and its standards and the terms and conditions
of the several layers of contracts, there would be no reason for a
decision to alter this pattern.

However, experience with the various titles of the ESEA—and,
particularly, Title I— has definitely demonstrated that quite often
the various levels of educational governance do not necessarily
perform in the best interests of the clients. Yet, under ESEA, if
the funds had been cut off as a result of inadequate performance
on the part of the educational institutions involved, the clients
would have suffered the loss of whatever benefits were trickling
down to them, such as a food program. And, inevitably, the clients
who would have suffered the most from such a funding cutoff
would have been the poor. Accordingly, there must be alternative
funding patterns spelled out in the legislation which can be employed that will serve the client in terms of his educational needs
—regardless of the performances of the institutions most readily
identified with such needs. In short, the federal contribution
should fund the client rather than the system; and the system—at
whatever level—should only receive federal funds as long as it is
adequately serving the clients. Therefore, the federal governance
agency should have full authority, in the event of clearly documented performance deficiencies and/or educational malpractice

on the part of an educational agency, to make use of funding patterns other than the primary one proposed. Schematized below are the funding alternatives proposed in relation to the primary funding pattern.

Proposed Patterns of Federal Funding

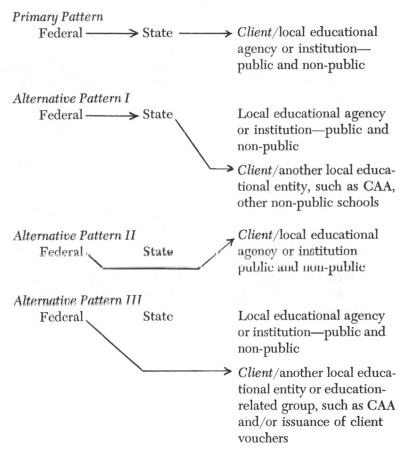

Primary Pattern
Federal ⟶ State ⟶ *Client*/local educational agency or institution— public and non-public

Alternative Pattern I
Federal ⟶ State | Local educational agency or institution—public and non-public
⟶ *Client*/another local educational entity, such as CAA, other non-public schools

Alternative Pattern II
Federal State | *Client*/local educational agency or institution public and non-public

Alternative Pattern III
Federal State | Local educational agency or institution—public and non-public
⟶ *Client*/another local educational entity or education-related group, such as CAA and/or issuance of client vouchers

With regard to all of the patterns, it is conceivable that the Federal Government might, at some point in time, be employing one or more of the alternatives simultaneously in any given state. For example, the contract with a particular local agency might be deemed as generally satisfactory by all its community client boards and their constituencies, and the primary funding pattern would continue. In contrast, within another agency of the same state, some or all of the boards and their constituencies might produce documentation that clearly reveals that agency's performance to be unsatisfactory in terms of the contracts. In the latter instance, an alternative funding pattern would be used in the event that the administrative appeals procedure—or even a lawsuit decided in favor of the clients—failed to produce corrective action by either the agency or the state. Alternative Pattern III represents the extreme in terms of inadequate institutional performance. Should this pattern become necessary, the federal contribution to both poor and non-poor clients would need to be greater than that under the other alternatives. The need for the increased contribution would be due to such factors as the loss of the state-local contribution and the necessity for the Federal Government to provide additional monies for developing the particular educational alternative involved. As with the other procedures described for the decision-making tactic, this procedure is also designed to contribute to the institutional accountability so critical to providing equal educational opportunity. And, in combination with the other tactics, the procedures of the decision-making tactic round out the leverage mechanisms needed to bring about the major revitalization of education for its clients, for the system at all levels, and for the nation as a whole.

With all of the tactics described, there is still one issue to be addressed; specifically, to what extent are these tactics likely to gain political acceptance. Had they been proposed in the early or middle 1960's, it is certain that their probability level for political acceptance would have hovered around zero. However, in the 1970's, it is our contention that the level for such acceptance is rising because of the need to deal pragmatically with a public institution that is financially precarious and also under challenge from its clients, segments of its professional constituencies, and the general public.

Specific indicators supporting this contention are most pronounced in the fiscal area. One is the decision of the California Supreme Court, *Serrano* v. *Priest*, on August 30, 1971, concerning financial inequities among school districts in that state. In this case, the court held "that the state equalization program 'partially alleviates the great disparities in local sources of revenue, but that the system as a whole generates school revenue in proportion to the wealth of the individual district.' "[3] The main precedent for this ruling was the "equal protection clause" of the Fourteenth Amendment to the U. S. Constitution. Perceiving public education as a right eligible for equal protection under this amendment, the judges stated that "education is the life line of both the individual and society" and that "today an education has become the *sine qua non* of useful existence."[4] The California decision has been followed by comparable rulings in Minnesota and Texas, and suits initiated in other states are likely to produce similar rulings.[5] Another indicator is the District Court decision in Washington, D. C., on May 25, 1971, *Hobson* v. *Board of Education*, which dealt with achieving equalization within a local school district (chapter 5). The court decisions have opened the door to state-wide and indistrict equalization of resources. What is now needed is national equalization. The combination of the proposed formula and the financial equity tactic provides a clear legislative route for equalization on a national basis—the clients have already found the judicial one on state and local bases.

Through such court decisions, the necessity for sweeping educational reforms is being signaled in the fiscal area. And the President's call for these reforms prior to any major funding of education is a further signal. However, the court decisions provide neither the mechanisms nor the funds necessary for the adequate and equitable financing of public education. Moreover, comparable reforms in the program areas have yet to appear on the horizon. While there has been a lot of activity, client demands have yet to exert any real leverage on the substance of the educational program. In view of the financial condition of education and the client demands for program change, the nation cannot wait for education to reform itself—a fact clearly demonstrated by the history of the education programs of the opportunity strategy and the necessity for outside legal intervention to correct state and local fiscal inequities. The tactics of the strategy being proposed here provide the necessary reform leverage in the fiscal, governance, and program areas. Federal intervention on behalf of the clients and the system which must serve them must be undertaken through the political process.

10

Politics and the
New National Strategy

FOR ITS FULFILLMENT, the national education strategy being proposed here depends upon the successful functioning of the political process, not only to bring the strategy into existence but also to create the administrative capability through which to implement it. From the standpoint of the political process, the key question for this or any other major strategy is its acceptability to the principal partners to the process—the President, the Congress, and the wide range of education's constituent groups, including the recently formed client-centered groups. Assuming national concern, which is already present, acceptability, in this instance, consists of a judicious and pragmatic use of several criteria: something for everyone, reform in behalf of equal educational opportunity, and the provision of sufficient resources over time within budget constraints. Accordingly, in this final chapter, the proposed new strategy for education is analyzed in terms of the several criteria for the successful functioning of the political process against the backdrop of national education politics during the 1970's. Also included is the rationale for the creation of a cabinet-level department of education. In analyzing the proposed strategy's political acceptability, we begin by looking at the President's recent involvement and anticipated role.

Presidential Leadership

Thus far, President Nixon's thrust in education has been a cautious one based on the uncertain condition of the educational system, the probability that major investment of federal funds in it would be unrewarding, and the problems with the federal budget. Nevertheless, the President, in two education messages to the Congress in 1970, pinpointed the two most critical needs of education. One was reform, which he stipulated as a condition for increased federal investment in education. The other was financial need, in which he recognized the inadequacies of existing sources of revenue and the inequities built into the allocation of these resources. In pinpointing these needs in the March 3, 1970, Message on Education Reform,[1] he also outlined part of his strategy for achieving the reform and dealing with school finance.

For his contingency of reform, he proposed the creation of a National Institute of Education within DHEW as a "first step toward reform" through providing "a coherent approach to research and experimentation." As rationale for this reform, the message cited the disappointing results from programs of compensatory education initiated by the preceding Administration— which Mr. Nixon proposed to continue but not to expand—and also called attention to the need for "new knowledge needed to make educational opportunity truly equal." Therefore, the new institute would have as its "first order of business" determining "what is needed—inside and outside of the school—to make our compensatory education effort successful." Since, as the message further pointed out, only one-half of one per cent of all public education budgets are devoted to research efforts (which then go unheeded by the schools), the system was going to have to learn how to innovate and what to change in order to realize the impact of this reform. In full agreement with the President on this reform measure, the Congress authorized the NIE in the Education Amendments of 1972.

In recognition of the financing problem, Mr. Nixon created the President's Commission on School Finance, which was also proposed in the March 3 message, and charged the commission with making a two-year study of revenue needs and fiscal priorities. While the new commission was asked to review disparities in expenditures among states and school districts, the suggestion in the message on funding sources for education was that federal monetary aid could most readily be achieved by federal revenue sharing with the states. Should revenue sharing be chosen as the solution, approximately two-fifths of the returned federal funds would probably go to education, but there would be no real assurance that this solution would fulfill the mounting needs of the systems, including the critical one of reform. Among its assignments, the commission was also asked to look at financial arrangements for the non-public schools, which educate 11 per cent of all pupils, for the purposes of promoting the fiscal solvency of these schools and of averting a new $4 billion cost to public education by their closing. In further recognition of the financing problem, the March 3 message reaches the point of the inevitable need for more "money." It then committed the Nixon Administration "to substantial increases in federal aid to education—to place this among the highest priorities in our budget . . . as we gain a new confidence that our education dollars are being wisely invested to bring back their highest return in social benefits. . . . As we get more education for the dollar, we will ask the Congress to supply many more dollars for education." Hence, the Administration has gone clearly on record as acknowledging the need for funds and an increased budget priority for elementary and secondary education.

Despite this acknowledgment, the Finance Commission produced a disappointing report in March 1972, in failing to answer the basic questions assigned to it concerning the source of revenue for education. Also, its principal recommendation—to place responsibility for funding the system on the states—was anticlimactic. This recommendation was an approach which the courts were already mandating in their assault on the local property tax as a main source of school revenue for elementary and secondary education.

The President's Message on Higher Education sent to the Congress on March 19, 1970, reemphasized the need of reforms in education, particularly in terms of meeting the financial needs of low-income, post-secondary students. As in the Message on Education Reform of March 3, President Nixon stressed the goal of "equal educational opportunity." He also revealed the nature of his reform strategy for higher education by outlining a major revamping and expansion of federal grants and loans with the specific intent of reversing the cited disparity between students from families of $15,000 income or more who attend college with nine times the frequency of their age peers from families of $3,000 income or less. Client-oriented reform was at least the heart of this message. A funding commitment was also extended to fulfill the proposed Higher Education Opportunity Act of 1970 aimed at consolidation and overhaul of legislation affecting higher education.

However, the net effect of the Administration's position on education has been a combination of deferral and of the maintenance of existing levels of funding under current program authorizations. Two years after the messages, there was little indication of a full strategy, spanning all levels of education, directly addressed to the two critical needs of education. The National Institute of Education is a component of such a strategy; the Commission on School Finance, a precursor to such a component. Only in the area of higher education do the indicators of a strategy emerge. In a speech on December 3, 1971, in which education was mentioned, Mr. Nixon revealed a search for new sources of revenue with which to achieve fiscal equity within education. In addition to a seeming lack of strategy, a further complication in the creation of a priority for education from the presidential standpoint is a deficit-ridden budget. Mr. Nixon would have a difficult time extracting a high priority for education from a budget that had so little flexibility possible in fiscal year 1973, and which also overlapped with a presidential election year. With regard to the budget, Mr. Nixon found his budgetary options to be more constrained than those which faced his predecessors in the early sixties.

At the same time that the Administration has proposed revenue sharing (emergency aid to desegregating districts having been enacted), it has also been cautiously pursuing its combined deferral–same-maintenance-level direction. In keeping with this direction, the equal educational opportunity proposals of the President in the spring of 1972 would combine ESEA Title I and Emergency School Assistance funding to provide limited resources of $300 per deprived child. Meanwhile, the problems within, and the pressure on, education have continued to escalate. Evidences of the self-initiated reform called for by the President as a contingency for increased funding have failed to materialize. Indeed, delayed funding of the system pending its reform—has been likened to asking a drowning man to learn how to swim better before throwing him a life preserver. In particular, the large city school systems are going bankrupt, as evidenced by New York City, Chicago, Philadelphia, Los Angeles, and others in their taking drastic measures, such as firing teachers, eliminating needed support services, and shortening the school year, to cut costs and stay within their budgets. State governments have proved unequal to the task—as the Detroit experience cited in chapter 7 illustrates—of rescuing the large city systems. The costs of education are rising as groups within the system, like teachers, demand salary increases and other benefits. And the demands for improved services coming from the clients and staff themselves will inevitably raise the costs of education, if the demands are to be realized. As if all of these problems are not enough, the states are confronted with court decisions, beginning with the California decision on *Serrano* v. *Priest* in August 1971, to undo their unequal fiscal systems for funding local school districts since they fail to comply with the equal protection provisions of the Fourteenth Amendment.

What all of these problems and pressures signal is the emergence of education as a major issue facing the Administration in the 1970's. Indeed, 1972 was certain to bring a renewed plea from the states for federal aid to offset the effects of internal state redistribution of funds, accompanied by a political drive for equalization among the states. In anticipation of such actions by the states, U. S. Education Commissioner Sidney P. Marland, Jr., publicly stated that the federal share of elementary and secondary school budgets must reach the 25 to 30 per cent level in this decade, and USOE produced an independent school finance study in 1971 to back up the Commissioner.[2] As a precedent to this ratio of federal fiscal responsibility, the Federal Government through the enactment of the Education Amendments of 1972 has legislated student financial aid which will result in federal financing of over one-fourth of the national costs of all higher education. Options for providing at least comparable treatment to the funding needs of preschool, elementary, and secondary education must now be considered—beginning with fiscal year 1974, and continuing in fiscal years 1975 and 1976.

In summary, the legislative proposals being made here for the enactment of a new strategy, including a bill of rights, a funding formula, and a set of educational reform tactics, address the two critical needs of education which have been identified by the President—reform and funding. As designed, the new strategy carefully intertwines these needs together. Moreover, through its formula, the strategy addresses the equalization task now being faced by the states, and it does so at all levels of educational development. In addition, the formula would, through its funding criteria on the cost of quality educational programs at each developmental level, provide sufficient funds to deal differentially with the needs of poor and non-poor clients. In this manner, the strategy meets the several political criteria of something for everyone, reform of the system, and the provision of sufficient resources over time.

In terms of presidential leadership, the new strategy offers a well-defined blueprint for rescuing both the clients and the system alike. The strategy offers to the educational system at its various governance levels sufficient funding and mechanisms for reform together, rather than in a causal sequence. It offers to the clients a guarantee of the right to an equal educational opportunity and the leverage on the system through which to achieve it. A negative response to the rescue of the clients and the system that must serve them can be sustained only if our society is willing to pay an outrageous price for welfare and crime. In order to compete in the struggle for a funding priority, the spokesmen for both the system and the clients must demonstrate to the Administration in the 1970's that public investment in education will yield the benefits of a productive society unburdened by dependency. If spokesmen from all facets of education can demonstrate the point, the Administration will probably take action, and submit proposals to the Congress for legislative enactment.

Congressional Initiative

For the proposed strategy or any other strategy to succeed, congressional action is required. As the policy-making arm of the Government, the Congress ultimately decides what education programs are to be sponsored at the federal level. And as the categorical history of USOE well attests, the Congress over the years has been particularly responsive to special needs in education. Some 130 separate education programs can now be identified in USOE alone, and there are about one-third that number scattered throughout 28 other federal agencies. Recent initiatives by the Congress, however, reveal a new tendency to look at broader issues than the narrow categories of the past and present. If this strategy can appeal to the developing concern with the broader issues of education as variously translated by the key House and Senate committees and, at the same time, can fulfill the several criteria identified as necessary for the successful functioning of the political process, the probabilities for the new strategy to gain acceptance become reasonably favorable. In particular, they seem favorable when the record of the 90th and 91st Congresses on education is examined. In this assessment of the probabilities for the proposed strategy being acceptable to the Congress, the educational activities of the House and Senate are separately analyzed, beginning with the Senate.

Senate action during the 90th and 91st Congresses has been particularly positive toward education. As evidenced in legislation, the Committee on Labor and Public Welfare under the chairmanship of Senator Claiborne Pell (Education Subcommittee) substantially revised and liberalized the ESEA Amendments of 1969 (passed in 1970) which resulted in an $8.3 billion annual authorization for fiscal year 1973 as contrasted with the fiscal year 1971 level of $5.5 billion. In the process of liberalizing the formula,

the Senate committee further modified the provisions of the legislation to add to the U. S. Commissioner of Education's authority
to monitor state and local performance, as illustrated by its "comparability" provisions, and also to give clients a much stronger
voice than before in the determination of how compensatory education funds were to be used in their behalf.

In addition to the ESEA amendments, the same Senate committee addressed the areas of higher education and early childhood
day care. For higher education, the Pell committee in 1971 wrote
a bill for student financial assistance, coupled with institutional
grant overrides, that exceeded the Administration proposals. The
bill reported by the House-Senate conference and signed by
President Nixon in June 1972 provided terms for granting substantially broadened federal assistance to both the institutions
of higher education and their students.

Complementing its concern for higher education, the Congress
has also shown a major interest in pre-school education, particularly for poor children. As the result of initiative from the same
Senate committee that produced the Pell bill of 1971, a comprehensive child development program with free day-care services to
poor families was passed by the Congress on December 7, 1971.
When the President vetoed the child development bill two days
later on the grounds of fiscal irresponsibility, he undoubtedly set
the stage for an intensified contest between the President and the
Congress for leadership on education legislation in 1972. In addition to the likelihood of intensifying this contest, both bills reflected the need for major federal intervention in education at
more than the elementary and secondary levels. Moreover, in their
respective areas, both bills revealed the tendency toward dealing
with broader issues than has been the case with most previous
education legislation.

Another sign of this tendency in the Senate is the Select Committee on Equal Educational Opportunity, chaired by Senator
Walter Mondale of Minnesota, which has been forging a new initiative for the Congress in the definition of equality and quality in
education. Some background on this committee is important because of its unusual and significant mandate. In its Senate au-

thorization of February 19, 1970, the committee was given investigative—rather than legislative—authority in order to provide
policy definitions as a foundation for future education legislation.
The composition of the committee has been deliberately designed
to provide a broad view of educational problems in the light of
other major interest areas, and particularly the courts. The committee's membership includes five members from the Senate Committee on Labor and Public Welfare, five from the Judiciary
Committee, and five Senators chosen at large. In terms of the
powerful southern bloc in the Senate, Senator John L. McClellan's
presence on the committee is a significant factor because of his
influential position on the Judiciary Committee. His avowal, during the initial Select Committee hearings, that he would fully support federal legislation that assured the best quality of education
to American children without "federal regimentation" of the
schools provided a positive note for the Select Committee's review
of the educational needs of deprived children.[3]

Chairman Mondale's interpretation of the committee's assignment is to take a broad view of "equal educational opportunity."
That is, he has refused to settle for equating equal educational
opportunity either with equality of education input resources—
such as overall dollar expenditures on a per capita basis, teacher
qualifications, and facilities—or with the mere exposure of the individual to an equal input of resources situation. Encompassing
both of these, he takes the view that the broader issue of educational outcomes for the individual is the key factor. In other words,
the provision of an equal educational opportunity can only really
be determined by what actually happens to the individual as a result of the program in the educational setting.

In outlining its own program of study, the Select Committee's
first "Interim Report" has given evidence that the Chairman's view
is prevailing, and that the committee would effectively deal with
the substantive issues of educational equality. In this report, the
committee recognized that an equal opportunity for quality education has not been achieved in any section of the country, and
studied a number of specific matters relating to it, such as the
relationships of educational opportunity and quality education to

housing patterns, employment opportunities, and racial imbalance, as well as the effectiveness of present provisions in the laws, such as ESEA and the Civil Rights Act of 1964, "with respect to racial imbalance and the possible need for modifications." Most importantly, the committee proposed to develop "a national policy in relation to quality education and racial isolation in the schools."[4]

If the Congress really faces up to the need for a national policy on "quality education and racial isolation" and the Mondale interpretation of the dimensions of equal educational opportunity prevails, then the nation will be taking a major step in the direction of fulfilling the Education Bill of Rights being proposed here. Within the Mondale committee, there has been substantial agreement that national policy has been lacking in this area and that the Congress has a duty to fill the policy void. While there will be obvious differences in reconciling liberal and conservative viewpoints on these issues, the key point is the recognized need for a consistent national policy. Since the committee's mandate was to produce a report and to recommend policy rather than to legislate or appropriate, it has a unique opportunity to provide clear-cut policy guidance, without the necessity of legislative compromise at the outset. Thus, through its committees and bills, the Senate has been heading into the substantive issues in the program area of education.

On the House side, the committees have also been actively engaged with education matters, but more from the fiscal standpoint than from the programmatic one. The House Education and Labor Committee under its Chairman, Carl Perkins of Kentucky, has, for the most part, been content to upstage the President both in terms of his legislative proposals and in the funding process, traditionally reserved to the powerful Committee on Appropriations. The House committee's strong sentiment for general aid to elementary and secondary education was manifested in the effort of a liberal bloc in the summer of 1971 to substitute a $5 billion general aid program for the President's proposals for emergency school assistance to facilitate school desegregation. This effort failed not so much for a lack of support within the committee, as for a lack of assurance that the general aid measure could pass the

House without Administration support. The membership of the House Education and Labor Committee is very strongly pro-education, but internal disagreements within the committee often prevent it from exercising unified leadership. Such disagreements lessen the likelihood of direct initiative from the House committee in the legislative area, but its favorable pattern of support for education programs, particularly in the fiscal area, makes it possible for it to react favorably to Presidential and Senate initiatives.

In the area of appropriations, the members of the House Education and Labor Committee have been instrumental in adding to the President's education budget for four successive years. In 1970 a liberal bipartisan bloc of the committee cooperated with the hastily formed Emergency Committee for the Full Funding of Education Programs to add a half-billion dollars to the President's education budget for fiscal year 1970—following his veto of the earlier addition of a billion dollars by the Congress. In the following three years, comparable sums were added to the education budget, this time with the full cooperation of the Committee on Appropriations. On the 1971 budget, an override of the Presidential veto was engineered in the House, but no such effort was needed on the 1972 budget since the President signed the bill. Both the House and the Senate, in committee and on the floor, added to the budget of the President for fiscal year 1973. From all of this activity, there emerged a clear picture of congressional intent on both the House and the Senate sides to create a political issue over education policy and legislative initiative. And as the political contest of popularity over education issues heated up between the President and the Congress in an election year, the liberals in the Congress were likely to use their record on education as a major weapon for political support in the campaigns, as well as in the halls of the Congress.

Summarizing in terms of the Congress, the proposed new strategy offers the promise of something for everyone in the financial area. And, as the formula is constructed, it contains a critical equalization factor that would favor the particularly hard-pressed southern group of states and the desperate large city school systems. In this sense, the strategy would offer general funding to the

states and local districts. However, the strategy through all of its
components—the Education Bill of Rights, the formula, and the
set of reform tactics—would condition the funds provided, to
make certain that the goal of equal educational opportunity for
the clients would be directly sought. Even in its beginning imple-
mentational stages, the formula, through its entitlements, would
presumably provide sufficient funding at each developmental level
of education to make a substantial difference to both clients and
system alike. The early 1970's are years of decision for education, and both the Congress and the President are fielding
pressure on assigning a priority to education. What the proposed
strategy offers is a concrete plan for fulfilling the priority that
should have appeal to both the executive and legislative branches.

However, the appeal of the strategy can really be assured if the
strategy can attract at least some general support from the lobbies
made up of the education professions, as well as support from the
more recently formed client-oriented ones. There is no doubt but
that the educational professions lobbies are searching for a new
priority for education. The key question for the strategy being
proposed here is whether or not it provides a priority that can gain
the support of the lobbies.

The Education Professions Lobbies

In assessing the chances of support for the proposed new strategy from a coalition of the lobbies, there is a common denominator
that lies at the heart of their pursuits—federal money—which provides a rationale for bringing the professional education associations together in the common cause of seeking a larger share of the
federal budget, and thereby a larger federal share of the total national education expenditure. A look at a few of the percentages
of the federal investment in education during the latter 1960's in
relation to the recent aspirations of some of the big lobbies reveals
the need for such a coalition.

Beginning with the acts of 1964, the federal contribution to national educational activities rose sharply until 1968 when it peaked.
Taking into account all educational levels, the federal contribution

reached 12.0 per cent of all educational expenditures in fiscal year
1968 as compared with 8.6 per cent in fiscal year 1964, but, by
fiscal year 1970, the total federal contribution to education had
slipped to 11.7 per cent.[5] In marked contrast to the slippage revealed by the percentages of the federal investment are the percentages being proposed by the lobbies. Representing elementary
and secondary education in general, the National Education Association has set a goal of 33 per cent as the legitimate federal
share for these levels, with the state and local agencies dividing
the balance.[6] At the higher education level, the potent American
Council on Education is looking beyond the one-third federal
share of institutional expenditures for instructional purposes, projected by Clark Kerr's study for the Carnegie Commission on
Higher Education.[7] Spokesmen for the higher education community have set their sights on 50 per cent as the needed federal share
of this expenditure.[8] Reversing the downward trend of the federal
investment in education most assuredly provides the common
ground for the professional education organizations to unite their
efforts at influencing national policy.

Indeed, there has been an effort in this direction. The lobbies
have found it possible to combine their quest for funds under ad
hoc procedures of the Emergency Committee for the Full Funding
of Education Programs (chapter 2), which has successfully pur
sued the limited objective of annual additions to the federal education appropriations. Built upon the common denominator of the
mutual need for money, the committee has produced a limited
cooperation among the associations and has achieved the status of
a tactical holding action in terms of the fiscal maintenance of existing politically acceptable programs. In so doing, the Full Funding
Committee has further shown that a combination of educational
interests can have a decided influence upon the outcome of congressional decisions. But what neither the committee nor any other
group, for that matter, has been able to do is to provide a spring-
board to an expanded cooperation on the larger issues of national
policy formulation and on legislative proposals for it.

One characteristic of the professional lobbies, which has stub-
bornly blocked the achievement of their enlarged cooperation, has

been their fragmented pursuit of limited special objectives. That
is, professional lobbies have worked most effectively with the
Congress when they promote the cause of a specific legislative
authorization, such as the Vocational Education Act (and its
amendments), Aid to Schools in Federally Affected Areas, Aid to
Public Libraries, Grants for Handicapped Children, Aid to Land
Grant Colleges, and so on. In these instances, the Congress has
had a clear picture of the aid that is being given and the special
constituency being favored, and the special lobbies can readily
organize behind the specific causes. The net result of this characteristic over the years has been to perpetuate the scores of legislative categories that now cover the educational landscape and to
produce a general state of fratricidal warfare among the groups
to gain attention and favor from the congressional committees,
since only a limited number of bills can be expected to pass in any
given session of the Congress. In turn, this fragmented pursuit of
limited special objectives has generally produced a strong status
quo influence on the educational system. Given the mandate of
producing federal support for the particular aims of special-interest constituencies, the overall result of this support is an increasing
entrenchment of these constituencies within the system. The problem is that the lobbies view themselves and their professional constituencies as the clients being favored by the various programs of
federal assistance, rather than the students for whom such constituencies presumably exist.

Thus, when the President called for major educational reform
in elementary and secondary education (March 3, 1970) and in
higher education (March 19, 1970), he made waves for the boats
floating the associations, as well as for the schools, on the political
process seas. Lacking substantive legislative proposals of their
own to present to the Congress and facing constituencies becoming restive with the lean years of educational financing from all
sources, the call for system reform has drawn an increasingly defensive reaction from the professional lobbies. They have failed
to grasp the point of the President's strong plea in behalf of an
equal educational opportunity for all persons, which ran through
the March 3 and March 19 messages. If they had caught it, they

might have realized that another common denominator, besides money, does indeed exist within the system—the students. If the associations could begin to form substantive positions based on the genuine "clients" of the system, they might find a new basis for cooperation.

An illustration of the associations' problem about who the real clients are occurred when the Senate Subcommittee on Education under Senator Pell was conducting its review and reporting out a bill (S. 659), dealing with assistance on higher education. Based largely on an extensive liberalization of the Nixon proposals for student financial assistance in 1971, Chairman Pell complained bitterly that he received "not a damn bit of help from the ACE" in getting his provisions through the committee and the Senate. And the Senator also criticized the council's lack of recognition of the need for reform in higher education. On the House side, Representatives Quie and Brademas also criticized the council for its inability to produce useful information to the House committee and then cited the council's insistence on taking rigid positions in favor of the institutional aid they were seeking, in preference to student aid.[9]

A similar doctrinaire position shackles the National Education Association in its resolve that "federal support to education be general in nature, and that these funds be allocated without federal control for expenditure and suballocation by state education agencies."[10] Being bound by such a resolution, the association cannot advance specific education programs which recognize the needs for system reform or the needs of the student clients within the system—even if some of their constituency and leadership were inclined to do so.

In fact, such doctrinaire positions are rapidly becoming untenable in the face of constituency demands for improved treatment in the public realm. Teachers are pushing militantly for higher salaries, for security, and for a better set of fringe benefits. The unit cost of education has risen at an unprecedented rate as the average cost per elementary and secondary pupil shot up from $375 in 1960 to $783 in 1970, an increase of 110 per cent.[11] Likewise, all educational expenditures as a share of the Gross

National Product increased from 5.1 per cent in 1960 to 7.6 per cent in 1970.[12] As education unit costs rise, the pressure on local education budgets has intensified, and professional organizations must compete to deliver the goods to their clientele. Thus, the labor-oriented American Federation of Teachers is managing to draw local teacher support away from the National Education Association by effective bargaining on teacher contracts, and thereby causing the latter organization to look around for new ground. Meanwhile, the local school systems are caught in the squeeze of unrelenting demands for professional benefits, rising client expectations, and unyielding local sources of funds to meet these demands. To illustrate further, local school bond elections in 1969 produced only 44 per cent of the dollar values voted on, as compared to 80 per cent in 1959.[13] At the state level, the governors are finding it impossible to gain new funds for education from their state treasuries. After four decades of steady growth, the state-level share of public school expenditures declined nationally from 39.4 per cent in 1958 to 38.5 per cent in 1968.[14] Thus, constituency pressure for various types of benefits is building upon the national associations at a time when educational resources at all levels are generally eroding.

As a result, the professional lobbies are now faced with the basic question of whether or not they can arrive at some common purpose that is acceptable not only to their constituencies but also to the President and the Congress—and possibly even to the student clients as well. Based on the financial crisis in education, their limited cooperation on the Emergency Committee for the Full Funding of Education Programs, and their individual association pronouncements, it is obvious that their collective preference is for the provision of unconditioned general aid at some substantial percentage level of the total national education expenditure. However, the experience with ESEA in the latter 1960's and the court decisions of the early 1970's that have revealed major fiscal inequities within education at both state and local levels suggest that neither the President nor the Congress will, despite the urgent need for increased funds for education, be willing to settle for this purpose as the definition of the priority of the 1970's. Indeed, it seems likely that this preference can now be classified as a political will-o'-the-wisp.

However, unconditioned federal funding, or general aid, is not the only basis on which the professional associations can arrive at a common purpose; the students within the system constitute another basis for cooperation. The question can then be raised as to whether or not the lobbies would be able to arrive at a common purpose which provides a salable and credible blending of concern for the student clients, the system, and their constituencies within it. In other words, the lobbies will very likely have to come to the realization that system reform in the direction of the genuine provision of equal educational opportunity for the student clients will be the price charged for a major new federal investment in the system. And it seems probable that if the pill of reform is coated with the sugar of sufficient funds to rescue the system, the lobbies may swallow it. The proposed new strategy, with its various component elements involving both funding and reform, provides the professional lobbies with just such an opportunity.

Indeed, if the professionals do not turn their attention to both the client and the system needs, they are likely to wake somewhere along the way and find that the President, the Congress, or the client-oriented lobbies have upstaged them in the educational rescue effort. For, in their own behalf, the client oriented groups have a potency which they are beginning to assess and which they may learn to invoke on national issues.

Client-oriented Lobbies

Historically, the professional associations have dominated the scene of advocacy for specific education programs before incumbent administrations, as well as with the Congress. In contrast, the client-oriented lobbies have often lacked the staff and sometimes the sophistication of the professional lobbies for continuous liaison on policy. Also, the client lobbies, such as the NAACP, the Urban Coalition, and the more recent Common Cause, have tended to focus on the general civil rights area, principally at the local level, rather than on education in particular. However, the situation is changing and the groups are beginning to focus on the sources of policy formulation in Washington to plead the cause of their clients within the system.

To illustrate, the Mississippi group representing the Delta Ministry made an impact on the Senate Committee on Public Welfare in their recitation of local abuses to ESEA Title I in June 1969 (chapter 2). In this connection, it is evident that some well-informed representatives of the clients, such as Ruby Martin of the Washington Research Project (NAACP-Legal Defense and Educational Fund), are able to provide the expert testimony to the congressional committees on client needs and to police the administration of funds at the federal level. Already cited (chapter 6), the work of the Washington Research Project in its review of the fiscal audits of ESEA Title I projects exposed local misuse of funds and, at the same time, exerted pressure on USOE to give its own publicity to audit findings, calling for the return of misused ESEA Title I funds from seven states in September 1971. Another client-oriented group, the National Welfare Rights Organization, had remarkable success in October 1970 in redirecting federal administrative policy with regard to using ESEA Title I funds for clothing the poor children, on the reasonable grounds that adequate clothing was a necessity for school attendance.

Still another group of great potential are the students of college age, who have now acquired the right to vote. At the campus level, student organizations, such as the National Student Association, have been cutting their organizational teeth on matters of institutional governance and program, as well as on the broad social issues of the Indo-China war and voting rights. While much of the student effort has been focused on campus concerns, there is significant evidence that the attainment of voting rights for eighteen-year-olds has shifted their attention to the national scene. Signaling this trend is the newly formed National Student Lobby, which by the summer of 1972 was representing 138 schools and a constituency of one million students. Its legislative goal for 1972 was that of funding $900 million for the new basic educational opportunity grants authorized by the Education Amendments of 1972, which the lobby worked to enact. Other concerns have included civil rights, civil liberties, the war, poverty, and the environment.[15] From such developments, it would appear that the students are clearly headed in the direction of participation in policy determinations on all matters which affect them. The extent to which the students will actually be able to influence national policy directly through either their organizations or their votes still remains to be seen. However, it is to be noted that there are national organizations, like Common Cause, that will cooperate with student organizations and other client-oriented groups on national issues.

As a "citizen lobby," Common Cause is of particular interest. Organized in August 1970 by John Gardner, former Secretary of DHEW and Director of the Urban Coalition from January 1968 to September 1970, Common Cause is directed at the revitalization of politics and government. It has worked successfully in the attainment of voting rights for eighteen-year-olds, and it is now very active in making these votes an influence for change in society. A main priority of the organization is to reform "the system," like that in education, so as to make it function in behalf of its clients. While the organization is aimed at middle-class memberships and lacks the singular cause of advocating the rights of poor people, it carries the potential for being a key element in coordinating the fragmented efforts at advocacy into a cohesive force for influencing the Congress and its legislative program. And, in fact, Gardner is determined to make federal legislation a primary focus of his cause.[16] In terms of Gardner's concern for education, Common Cause has a major role to play in advancing the cause of a new education mandate. It could become the catalyst for bringing together the diverse views of many segments of society in an uncommon coalition for citizen-oriented legislation by the Congress.

At this time, no definitive diagram of the process with which the client-oriented groups might manage to cooperate in behalf of a national strategy for education can be drawn. For such cooperation to occur, it will take organization, dedication, and a lot of planning by some party or committee to bring about a concerted

national focus for these varied groups on national education matters. However, it seems likely that the client groups will seek to
have an impact on education policy and legislative initiative, and
it would be very much in the interest of the professional lobbies to
get in touch with them. Ruby Martin and John Gardner are
within easy walking distance of the National Education Association and the American Council on Education in the Dupont Circle
area of Washington. Since education is heating up as a political
issue at the local, state, and federal levels as a result of its increasingly urgent and visible needs, neither the professional nor
the client-oriented lobbies are likely to overlook education in the
early 1970's. Thus, while a coalition of a majority of the lobbies is
improbable, it seems reasonable to suggest that a major legislative
proposal for education, such as the one being advanced here,
would attract their interest and support for a variety of reasons.

When the various political forces influencing national education
policy do manage "to put it all together" in behalf of advocacy for
a new education mandate in which the federal role will inevitably
increase, the issue of the adequacy of existing federal arrangements to administer such a mandate will inevitably become a matter for serious attention. For not only must the political process
initially and subsequently function in successful ways with regard
to the new mandate, but there must also be an administrative
structure which is adequate to the discharge of the expanded
concept of the federal role being proposed.

Administrative Governance

Both for the kind of program and for the expanded federal role
that would emerge from the strategy being proposed here, the
question that must inevitably be asked is, to what extent are the
present federal administrative arrangements sufficient to the task?
Since the new strategy—in its legislative proposals for an Education Bill of Rights, a formula, and a set of reform tactics—en-
visages program consolidation as well as expansion in the federal
role, the combined impact of this new involvement would sig-

nificantly increase the demands upon the Federal Government for administrative leadership. Among these demands would be such key ones as the management of the sharply enlarged federal investment generated by the formula, the interfacing of existing educational programs with the new program for the provision of equal educational opportunity, the enforcement of performance requirements in relation to the federal investment and Education Bill of Rights, and the utilization of diverse technical assistance from the private and public sectors in all areas and at all levels of the program. In answer to the question then, such demands will necessitate major changes in the existing federal administrative arrangements for the successful discharge of this or any other major education strategy that is directed at education's revitalization through reform and funding. As rationale for the changes being proposed, an analysis of the problems inherent in the existing arrangements is presented in conjunction with a recommendation for a new administrative arrangement.

USOE, as the main component of the federal education arrangements, has never been endowed with the administrative powers commensurate with its responsibilities to all of its many clients. Historically, it has been—and is—a creature of congressional and presidential power politics, in which the contest has been a three-cornered one of seeking ways to pump funds into the educational system to accomplish a specific and worthy objective, to leave the local scene undisturbed in terms of performance responsibility, and to endow USOE with only that amount of authority essential for assuring the proper distribution of the funds to the system. Rarely does USOE even gain enough staff to do a creditable job of administering the sizable grant funds that are generously given by the Congress to its favorite categories. The result of this contest over the years has been the establishment of a very low profile for USOE in terms of its supervisory powers over federal programs in the system.

Thus, when the Administration or the Congress decides to launch a significant new national program in education which calls for direct federal control over program design and execution by local agencies, the inclination has been to assign the responsibilities to the National Science Foundation, the Office of Economic Opportunity, or to some other part of DHEW, like the National Institutes of Health or the new NIE. The National Science Foundation and the Office of Economic Opportunity have been given mandates which permitted them broad discretion in the area of program design, as well as much broader appropriation authority and staff support to carry out the mandates, such as a new science curriculum for the schools or a preschool program for poor children. In contrast, USOE has been assigned explicit legislative mandates with very limited powers of discretion which consist of the authority to grant funds to eligible agencies and to preside over the distribution of these funds. When it has been given discretionary authority in rare cases, like research, USOE has been hobbled by appropriation cuts, coupled with external guidance from the Office of Management and Budget and the Congress on how best to employ the funds. Never having been entrusted with major discretionary funds, USOE has gained the reputation of being a funding agency which lacks the power to affect educational outcomes in substantive ways.[17] In short, USOE, in its present form, would be unable to administer the proposed education mandate.

Indeed, it is this history of inherent weakness that prompted President Nixon to propose in his messages of March 1970 that two new education agencies be created within DHEW to bring new strength to the federal education structure. A National Institute of Education was proposed to subsume the entire field of educational research and development, and a National Foundation for Higher Education was proposed to initiate the development of innovative approaches to post-secondary education. Both of these new agencies would be endowed with broad grants of authority over program design, as well as with generous funding and flexibility for high-level staff appointments. Also, both would be independent of USOE, but would report to the Commissioner of Education. These changes would, of course, upgrade the DHEW education structure and add to its discretionary funding capability, and they would enhance the status of the Commissioner of Education. Moreover, the net effect of these changes would presumably add to the capability of DHEW to affect educational outcomes for people. In the Education Amendments of 1972, the Congress affirmed the Institute, rejected the Foundation, and created a new Assistant Secretary of Education to supervise both NIE and USOE.

However, these changes would not create a federal agency with the power to administer a broad new mandate of educational improvement, such as the one being proposed here. There are some fundamental administrative problems that require stronger measures than those thus far proposed, if a new national strategy for education is to become a reality. These problems are examined, in turn, as part of the rationale for a new cabinet-level department of education.

DEALING WITH STATES

As an integral part of the educational establishment, USOE has been locked into a mold in elementary and secondary education of dealing solely with chief state school officers and, through them, with local school superintendents. For the area of vocational education, the state relations are with the state boards for vocational education, which are sometimes not a part of the state educational agency. In higher education, the relations are with college and university presidents. Legally bound to these formal relations, USOE has had practically no leverage on higher or alternative levels of authority, like governors, mayors, and non-educational boards and agencies, through which to issue and enforce policies that would require changes in the performance traditions of the existing educational agencies. In effect, USOE has had no recourse but to gain as much performance and compliance as it can wring from well-entrenched local educational authorities.

Under the proposed strategy, the Federal Government would have the option to deal with higher-level state and local authorities, instead of with the regular educational authorities at those levels, to bring about increased performance and compliance. And the Government would also have the option of calling upon non-educational agencies for selected programmatic services. For example, it should be feasible for the federal agency to negotiate preschool services with welfare agencies or an adult education program with private agencies, when the regular educational system is lacking in such capabilities. Also, the federal agency should have negotiating powers with state governors that permit agreements on how educational services can best be rendered in a given state for public and non-public school students and how best to achieve compliance with policies. In order to negotiate at these levels, cabinet status is required to provide the necessary political flexibility and leverage, a status which USOE has never acquired but which the federal agency would need as a part of the proposed national strategy. In this connection, it is unrealistic to assume that internal rearrangements within DHEW would endow USOE with new authority and prestige of the magnitude required to carry out the proposed new mandate.

RELATIONS WITH THE CONGRESS

At the national level, a comparable problem of negotiating powers is involved. The Congress has historically kept a close watch on the affairs of USOE through its legislative and appropriations committees. USOE authority is usually conferred by law on the Commissioner of Education, rather than on the Secretary of DHEW, and the USOE appropriations are likewise made directly to the commissioner. In fiscal year 1971, the appropriations committees saw fit to break the USOE funds away from the rest of DHEW and to include them in a separate bill—primarily to expedite their passage through the Congress. Moreover, the committees tend to liaise directly with the commissioner and other USOE officials on the specifics of bills and on the administration of funds. Thus, in some ways, the Commissioner of Education is accorded the de facto status of a secretary.

However, the commissioner lacks both the authority and the prestige of a cabinet secretary when it comes to speaking on Administration policy before the Congress. His position is always that of having to defer decision-making to the Secretary of DHEW, who, in turn, has access to the President and to the Director of the

Office of Management and Budget. If a commissioner falls out of favor with the Administration, as James E. Allen, Jr., did in 1970, USOE becomes extremely vulnerable to external intrusion into its affairs. When a commissioner earns full Administration support, as Sidney P. Marland, Jr., did in 1971, USOE fortunes tend to rise with the tide. Hence, both the office of the commissioner and USOE, in general, acquire more status from the personal effectiveness of, and political support for, the incumbent commissioner than from their administrative placement in the governmental scheme of things. And the result for both is a corresponding lack of status and stability that go with a cabinet-level department.

RELATIONS WITH THE PRIVATE SECTOR

Still another problem that has confronted USOE and its commissioners has been the one of inadequate relations with the private sector. This inadequacy, in large part, can be attributed, however inadvertently, to the size of USOE's professional constituency. To explain, this constituency—consisting of 50 state agencies, 18,000 local districts, 2,000 colleges and universities, scores of private associations, 2 million teachers, and 60 million students—fully dominates the attention of the commissioner and his associates. Every Commissioner of Education has been overwhelmed with the time problem of coping with this constituency in terms of official business and ceremonial attention. USOE lacks the capability—and the commissioner the time—to relate to the private non-educational sector of our society; USOE has become completely one-sided in its orientation to the education profession. As one consequence, USOE is unable to provide effective leadership to its vast constituency in the utilization of new developments in technology, such as computers and telecommunications. As another consequence, USOE is unable to participate effectively in matters which affect consumers and labor, like new manpower training needs and industrial research developments. Also contributing to the problem with the private sector has been the agency's inadequate prestige, compounded of an insufficient staff capability and a lack of top-level policy involvement. Cabinet-level status would facilitate these relations, which would be essential to the strategy being proposed here.

PRIORITIES AT THE FEDERAL LEVEL

At the federal agency level, education has problems that have resulted in its being at a competitive disadvantage on priorities, both within and outside DHEW. And DHEW itself has a unique problem with its budget priorities. Within the federal budget totals, it now ranks as the second largest among the departments and the fastest-growing. Both its size and growth make it a special target for restraints from the Office of Management and Budget trying to cope with a deficit budget. DHEW budget obligations jumped from approximately $6.5 billion in 1955 to approximately $64.5 billion in 1971—a tenfold increase.[18] The spectacular increase has resulted from the growth of what are classified as its "noncontrollable" expenditures, such as social security payments, public assistance, and medicare, which, by law, require the Federal Government to pay sums to its beneficiaries whenever they are eligible for them. In total, these amounts have risen from $5.8 billion to $55.8 billion during the period cited above, and they now represent some 87 per cent of all DHEW appropriations. Education represented $3.7 billion of the 1971 total (5.8 per cent), and education reached its peak of 9.7 per cent of the DHEW total in fiscal year 1967.[19] A major impediment affects education within DHEW in that it lies completely within the 13 per cent margin of the DHEW budget which is classified as "controllable" and which therefore must absorb the shock of ceilings imposed on the DHEW total budget by the Office of Management and Budget. In the crunch of deficit control ceiling limits, DHEW simply lacks the flexibility to grant significant budget increases to education. And in the push and shove of DHEW priorities, education looms as a "deferrable" commodity in contrast to the "now" requirements of medical care and welfare. Thus, even education-oriented Secretaries, like Elliot Richardson and John Gardner with their long records of support of education, found their options in this area severely limited.

When it comes to interagency competition, education has still other problems. In this arena, USOE competes with agencies, like the National Science Foundation and the Office of Economic Opportunity, for legislative and budget authority. Government-wide, USOE shares the federal education budget with DHEW and 28 other departments and agencies—with USOE having 36 per cent of the budget; other areas of DHEW, 16 per cent; and 48 per cent going to the remaining agencies.[20] A share of the larger programs is variously assigned to agencies, like the Veterans Administration (12 per cent) and Defense (8 per cent), as a part of carrying out other federal missions. And, as already noted, the significant discretionary programs affecting education generally are administered by the National Science Foundation, the Office of Economic Opportunity, and by a third group in the Department of the Interior (Indian education). In this regard, when Head Start was transferred to DHEW in 1969, it was not placed in USOE; instead, it became the nucleus for an Office of Child Development in the Office of the Secretary of DHEW. Thus, child development, by DHEW definition, is not regarded as a part of education—at least as exemplified by USOE. Moreover, it is evident that USOE suffers from the reputation—whether earned or assigned—of lacking the administrative style to operate programs which entail innovation or direct service to clients. Regardless of the causality of this reputation, the federal education structure is weakened by it, and weakness of any kind would undermine the proposed new strategy for education.

In this presentation of the rationale for the creation of a new cabinet-level department of education, two additional points must be included. One is that such an agency would provide a sound basis for the consolidation of those education programs at the federal level which relate to general public needs, as contrasted with those serving special federal missions for defense, veterans, and agriculture. The proposed inclusions would embrace all education programs within DHEW, as well as those now assigned to the Departments of Interior and Housing and Urban Development and those of the National Science Foundation and the Office of Economic Opportunity. On the basis of the federal budgets of these programs for fiscal year 1972, a total of $8.5 billion would be available to the proposed department of education, which would exceed the sums separately budgeted for seven other cabinet departments in that year.[21] Through these combinations, the new department would more readily generate the resources, authority, and capability to administer the proposed education mandate than would be possible under the existing arrangements.

The other point is simply stated—education is too important a function in today's society to be relegated to a subordinate role. In making this statement, it is to be underscored that we do not subscribe to the frequently raised charge that DHEW is ungovernable, since this charge has been consistently refuted by the excellent records of strong Secretaries, like Fleming, Gardner, Cohen, and Richardson. For the maximum impact to be achieved from the program consolidation and the proposed new strategy, the currently existing federal education structure is insufficient to the magnitude of the task that would be involved. Indeed, it is time that education becomes recognized at the national level as the enormously significant contributor to the nation's continued growth and well-being that it can and must be. Neither the clients nor the nation should any longer be considered as "deferrable." It is time that education arrives permanently in the governance structure of our society. Cabinet status is thus an essential component of the proposed strategy for education. Not only is the political process needed to create—and then to sustain—a major new strategy, but a new federal administrative arrangement is also needed to guarantee the success of this strategy.

A Concluding Note

For the continued well-being of the nation as a whole, it is time that the potential of education as an individually and collectively liberating force in society be recognized. That is the direction in which the partial education strategies of the 1960's were heading. If they have faltered because too much was wrong with their assumptions, which in turn flawed their designs, these strategies have nevertheless illuminated the rightness of their direction. In so doing, they have also illuminated the several key requirements for a new strategy—an equal educational opportunity must become a legally protected right for every citizen, what is wrong must be corrected, and the resources provided must be both adequate and sufficiently conditioned so as to guarantee each citizen's right. If the whole nation is ever to benefit from the realization of education's full potential, then these requirements must become translated through the political process into a strategy that will see this potential become a reality.

For any strategy, including this one, to realize this goal fully will take time. The experience with the partial strategies of the 1960's can be viewed as the first step. The design for a strategy that has been proposed here could become a second one. However, this second step waits upon the successful functioning of the political process. It may be that this process will be initiated by the Administration in the early 1970's for the legislative attainment of the historic and still elusive goal of equal educational opportunity. It is our belief that the mandate for this goal will occur in the 1970's. And when it does, education will have come of age as a liberating force for the clients, the system, and the nation.

APPENDIX A

EXCERPTS FROM
PUBLIC LAW 89–10, 89th CONGRESS, H. R. 2362, APRIL 11, 1965
TO IDENTIFY THE TWO THRUSTS IN TITLE I's STATEMENT OF MISSION

AN ACT

To strengthen and improve educational quality and educational opportunities in the Nation's elementary and secondary schools.

Be it enacted by the Senate and House of Representatives of the United States of America in Congress assembled, That this Act may be cited as the "Elementary and Secondary Education Act of 1965."

TITLE I—FINANCIAL ASSISTANCE TO LOCAL EDUCATIONAL AGENCIES FOR THE EDUCATION OF CHILDREN OF LOW-INCOME FAMILIES AND EXTENSION OF PUBLIC LAW 874, EIGHTY-FIRST CONGRESS

✻   ✻   ✻   ✻   ✻

DECLARATION OF POLICY

child benefit ⎰ SEC. 201. In recognition of the special educational needs of children of low-income families and the impact that concentration of low-income families have on the ability of local educational agencies to support adequate educational programs, the Congress hereby declares it to be system benefit

> the policy of the United States to provide financial assistance (as set forth in this title) to local educational agencies serving areas with concentrations of children from low-income families to expand and improve their educational programs by various means (including preschool programs) which contribute particularly to meeting the special educational needs of educationally deprived children.

❖   ❖   ❖   ❖   ❖

APPLICATION

system benefit

> SEC. 205 (a) A local educational agency may receive a basic grant or a special incentive grant under this title for any fiscal year only upon application therefor approved by the appropriate State educational agency, upon its determination (consistent with such basic criteria as the Commissioner may establish)—
> (1) that payments under this title will be used for programs and projects (including the acquisition of equipment and where necessary

child benefit

> the construction of school facilities) (A) which are designed to meet the special educational needs of educationally deprived children in school attendance areas having high concentrations of children from low-income families and (B) which are of sufficient size, scope, and quality to give reasonable promise of substantial progress toward meeting those needs, and nothing herein shall be deemed to preclude two or more local educational agencies from entering into agreements, at their option, for carrying out jointly operated programs and projects under this title;

child benefit {
(2) that, to the extent consistent with the number of educationally deprived children in the school district of the local education agency who are enrolled in private elementary and secondary schools, such agency has made provision for including special educational services and arrangements (such as dual enrollment, educational radio and television, and mobile educational services and equipment) in which such children can participate. . . .

✤   ✤   ✤   ✤   ✤

APPENDIX B

Mr. Charles Lee   February 10, 1970
  Emergency Committee for the Full
  Funding of Education Programs

Mr. Samuel Halperin   February 16, 1970
  Education Services Seminar

Mrs. Ruby Martin   February 17, 1970
  Washington Research Project

Mr. August Steinhilber   February 24, 1970
  National School Boards Association

Dr. Joseph Tanner   February 27, 1970
Dr. Joseph L. Mazur
Mr. Jack Nairus
  Cleveland Public Schools

Congressman John Brademas   March 2, 1970
  House Committee on Education and Labor

Sen. Walter Mondale   March 19, 1970
  United States Senate

Mr. J. Graham Sullivan   March 30–31, 1970
Mr. Henry Boas
Mrs. Josie Bain
Mr. William Anton
  Los Angeles City School Districts

Mr. John Lumley   April 22, 1970
National Education Association

Mr. Jack Morse   May 14, 1970
American Council on Education

Mr. Ken Young   May 19, 1970
Legislative Counsel, AFL–CIO

Mr. Peter P. Muirhead   May 21, 1970
Associate Commissioner for Higher Education, USOE

Mr. Thomas Rosica   May 28–29, 1970
Mr. Milton Goldberg
Philadelphia City School District

Mr. James F. Kelly   July 13, 1970
Assistant Secretary-Comptroller, HEW

Mr. Emery F. Bacon   July 14, 1970
Federal Interagency Committee on Education (telephone)

Mr. Jon Goldstein   August 12, 1970
Social Security Administration

Dr. Alexander Astin   August 24, 1970
American Council on Education

Dr. Alice M. Rivlin   August 24, 1970
Brookings Institution

Mr. James Moore   August 26, 1970
Division of Student Financial Aid, USOE

Mr. David A. Johnson   August 26, 1970
Talent Search, BHE-USOE

Dr. Leonard H. O. Spearman   August 26, 1970
Division of Student Special Services, BHE-USOE

Miss Mollie Orshansky   September 2, 1970
Social Security Administration

Mr. John Lagomarcino   September 9, 1970
Common Cause

Mr. Rodney E. Leonard   September 17, 1970
The Children's Foundation

Dr. Robert L. Egbert   September 18, 1970
  Follow Through Program, USOE

Mr. Jerry Brader   September 18, 1970
  Division of Student Financial Aid, USOE

Mr. Charles L. Schultze   September 21, 1970
  Brookings Institution

Mr. Bill Briggs and Mrs. Susan Orr   October 1, 1970
  National Welfare Rights Organization

Mr. Douglass Cater   October 2, 1970
  Formerly Special Assistant to the
  President of the United States

Mr. Gerald Sronfe   October 5, 1970
  National Committee for the Support
  of the Public Schools

Mr. John Gardner   October 30, 1970
  Former Secretary of HEW
  Chairman, Common Cause

NOTES

CHAPTER 2

1. Adam Yarmolinsky, "The Beginnings of OEO," in *On Fighting Poverty*, ed. James L. Sundquist (New York: Basic Books, Inc., 1969), pp. 34–35.

2. James L. Sundquist, *Politics and Policy* (Washington, D. C.: The Brookings Institution, 1968), p. 216.

3. Lyndon B. Johnson, *Public Papers of the President, January 1–May 31, 1965* (Washington, D. C.: U. S. Government Printing Office, 1968), p. 407.

4. Ibid., pp. 412–413.

5. Ibid., p. 415.

6. Ibid., pp. 1013–1014.

7. National Advisory Council on the Education of Disadvantaged Children, *Annual Report to the President, March 30, 1966* (Washington, D. C.: USOE, 1966).

8. *National Conference on Education of the Disadvantaged, July 1966* (Washington, D. C.. USOE publication OE-37004).

9. *Public Papers of the President*, p. 407.

10. Interview with Mr. Douglas Cater, October 2, 1970.

11. Interview with Mr. John Gardner, October 30, 1970.

12. Sundquist, *Politics and Policy*, p. 211.

13. Gardner interview, October 30, 1970.

14. Sundquist, *Politics and Policy*, pp. 211–216.

15. USOE, "Program Review of the State of Mississippi under Title I, Elementary and Secondary Education Act of 1965" (USOE/DCE), July–August 1969.

16. U. S. Congress, Senate Committee on Labor and Public Welfare, *Report on the Elementary and Secondary Education Amendments of 1969*, 91st Congress, 2d session, 1970, Senate Report 91–364, p. 10.

17. Washington Research Project, *Title I of ESEA: Is It Helping*

Poor Children? (New York: NAACP Legal Defense and Educational Fund, Inc., 10 Columbus Circle, 1969).

CHAPTER 3

1. Washington Research Project, *Title I of ESEA: Is It Helping Poor Children?* (New York: NAACP Legal Defense and Educational Fund, 1969).
2. Stephen K. Bailey and Edith K. Mosher, *ESEA: The Office of Education Administers a Law* (Syracuse, N.Y.: Syracuse University Press, 1968). See discussion, chapter III, pp. 72–97.
3. U. S. Congress, House Committee on Appropriations, *Hearings on Supplemental Appropriations for Departments of Labor and HEW, for fiscal year 1966*, 89th Congress, 1st session, 1965, p. 205.
4. Ed. Note: Senior Author's experience with the USOE administration of ESEA Title I is the basis for most of the incidents described.

CHAPTER 4

1. See James L. Sundquist, *Politics and Policy* (Washington, D. C.: The Brookings Institution, 1968), pp. 155–195.
2. Telephone conversation with Mr. Francis Keppel, January 1970.
3. Gary Orfield, *The Reconstruction of Southern Education* (New York: John Wiley & Sons, 1969), p. 186.
4. David Rogers, *110 Livingston Street* (New York: Random House, 1968). See Introduction, chapter IX, and chapter XIII.
5. National Advisory Council on State Departments of Education, *The State of State Departments of Education*, Fourth Annual Report (Washington, D. C.: U. S. Government Printing Office, 1969), p. 10.
6. Ibid., p. 3.
7. Ibid., p. 3.
8. Stephen K. Bailey and Edith K. Mosher, *ESEA: The Office of Education Administers a Law* (Syracuse, N.Y.: Syracuse University Press, 1968), pp. 53–55.
9. U. S. Congress, House Committee on Government Operations, *Operations of the Office of Education, Hawaiian Seminars*, 90th Congress, 2d session, 1968, House Report No. 1572.
10. Southern Education Reporting Service, *Statistical Summary of School Segregation–Desegregation in the Southern and Border States, 1965–66* (Nashville, Tennessee, December 1965), pp. 10, 12.
11. "ESEA Title I Program Guide No. 28" (USOE/DCE), February 27, 1967.
12. "Program Review of the State of Mississippi under Title I Elementary and Secondary Education Act of 1965" (USOE/DCE), July–August 1969.

Chapter 5

1. "Reading Improvement Program, Title I Evaluation," Cleveland Public Schools, Division of Research and Development, October 1969.
2. Interview with Dr. Joseph Mazur, Cleveland, February 27, 1970.
3. Interview with Dr. Josie Bain and Mr. Henry Boas, Los Angeles, March 30, 1970.
4. Interview with Mr. Thomas Rosica, Philadelphia, May 28–29, 1970.
5. "Program Review of the State of Mississippi under Title I ESEA" (USOE/DCE), July–August 1969.
6. Complaint in the United States District Court for the Northern District of Mississippi, Delta Division, *Willie Reed Taylor, et al.* v. *the Coahoma County School District, et al.*, Civil Action No. DC698, February 21, 1969.
7. Ibid., Amendments to Complaint, dated April 9, 1969.
8. "Program Review" (USOE/DCE), Statistical Evaluation of Comparability, 1967–68 School Year.
9. "Program Review" (USOE/DCE).
10. United States District Court for the District of Columbia, *Hobson* v. *Hanson*, Civil Action No. 82–66, Circuit Judge Wright, Findings of Fact, pp. 50–51.
11. Ibid., and California Supreme Court, *Serrano* v. *Priest*, August 30, 1971.

Chapter 6

1. *A Report of the Third Year of Title I ESEA*, (Washington, D. C.: USOE publication OE–37021–68, 1969), pp. 20–21.
2. Wilson C. Riles (chairman), *The Urban Education Task Force Report* (New York: Praeger Publishers, 1970). See pp. 159–183.
3. U. S. Congress, Senate Committee on Labor and Public Welfare, *ESEA Amendments of 1969*, 91st Congress, 2d session, Senate Report 91–634, p. 166.
4. *The Urban Education Task Force Report*, pp. 269–272.
5. Ibid., pp. 216–224, and Washington Research Project, *Title I of ESEA: Is It Helping Poor Children?* (New York: NAACP Legal Defense and Educational Fund, 1969), p. 104.
6. USOE/DCE, "Focus on Follow Through," March 1970.
7. President Lyndon B. Johnson, *Message to the Congress on the District of Columbia, March 13, 1968* (Washington, D. C.: U. S. Government Printing Office, 1968).
8. USOE, Anne O. Hughes, "Status Report on the Anacostia Community School Project," September 1970.

9. *The Urban Education Task Force Report,* pp. 268–269.

10. USOE, negotiations between the senior author as Director, Division of Compensatory Education, and Ewald B. Nyquist, Deputy Commissioner for the State of New York, spring 1968.

11. USOE Memorandum to Chief State School Officers from U. S. Commissioner of Education Harold Howe II, June 1, 1968.

12. USOE, "ESEA Title I Program Guide No. 54," 1969.

13. USOE, "Program Review of the State of Mississippi under Title I ESEA" (USOE/DCE), July–August 1969: Letter to Garvin H. Johnston from James E. Allen, Jr., July 9, 1969.

14. Ibid.: Letter to Garvin H. Johnston from James E. Allen, Jr., August 26, 1969.

15. U. S. Congress, Senate Committee on Labor and Public Welfare, *Report on the ESEA Amendments of 1969,* 91st Congress, 2d session, p. 10.

CHAPTER 7

1. U. S. Congress, Senate Select Committee on Equal Educational Opportunity, *Hearings,* Part 1A, 91st Congress, 2d session, May 12, 1970, p. 322.

2. Ibid., Testimony of Mark R. Shedd, Superintendent of Schools, Philadelphia, September 21, 1971.

CHAPTER 9

1. John E. Coons, William H. Clune III, and Stephen D. Sugarman, "Educational Opportunity: A Workable Constitutional Test for State Financial Structures," *California Law Review* (April 1969), p. 340.

2. Ibid., pp. 340–345.

3. *Education Daily* (Washington, D. C.: Capitol Publications), September 3, 1971, p. 4.

4. Ibid., p. 5.

5. Peter Milius, *Washington Post,* October 16, 1971.

CHAPTER 10

1. President Richard Nixon, Message to the Congress, *Message on Education Reform, March 3, 1970* (Washington, D. C.: U. S. Government Printing Office, March 1970).

2. *Future Directions for School Financing: National Educational Finance Project* (Gainesville, Florida, 1971), chapter VII, pp. 33–38.

3. U. S. Congress Senate Select Committee on Equal Educational Opportunity, *Hearings,* Part 1A, 91st Congress, 2d Session, April 21, 1970, p. 102.

4. U. S. Congress, Senate Select Committee on Equal Educational Opportunity, *Interim Report* (Committee Print), September 1970, p. x.

5. USOE, Estimated Expenditures by Regular and "Other" Educational Institutions, by source of funds, United States, 1959–60 to 1969–70 (unpublished tables, 1970).

6. Interview with Mr. John Lumley, 'National Education Association, April 22, 1970.

7. Clark Kerr, *New Levels of Federal Responsibility for Higher Education*, Carnegie Commission on Higher Education (New York: McGraw-Hill, 1968), p. 8.

8. Interview with Mr. Jack Morse, American Council on Education, May 14, 1970.

9. *The Chronicle of Higher Education*, V, no. 37 (Washington, D. C., August 2, 1971).

10. National Education Asssociation, The Resolutions of the National Education Asssociation of the United States (mimeographed draft; Washington, D. C., 1971), Resolution C-20d.

11. USOE, *Digest of Educational Statistics, 1970* (Washington, D. C.: U. S. Government Printing Office, 1970), p. 58, Table 77.

12. Ibid., p. 21, Table 25.

13. Ibid., p. 53, Table 71.

14. Ibid., p. 53, Table 70.

15. *The New York Times*, Sunday, March 26, 1972.

16. John Gardner, Common Cause, interview, October 30, 1970.

17. U. S. Congress, Senate Committee on Labor and Public Welfare, Report on S. 659, 92d Congress, 1st Session, Report 92–554, pp. 60–67.

18. Charles L. Schultze, *Setting National Priorities: The 1971 Budget* (Washington, D. C.: The Brookings Institution, 1970), p. 56.

19. Ibid.

20. U. S. Office of Management and Budget, Special Analyses, *Budget of the United States Government, Fiscal Year 1972* (Washington, D. C.: U. S. Government Printing Office, 1971), p. 120, Tables 1–3.

21. Ibid.

INDEX

Advisory committees, 113–16
Advocacy concept, 109–10; and Title
I, 41, 44; types of advocates, 110
AFDC (Aid for Dependent Children), 18, 19, 24
Agriculture, Department of, 124
Aid to Land Grant Colleges, 206
Aid to Public Libraries, 206
Aid to Schools in Federally Impacted
Areas, 206. See also Federal impact aid
Alabama, 42, 59
Allen, James E., Commissioner of Education, 52, 116, 117, 130, 217;
issues Title I program guide, 56;
calls for Mississippi Title I program review, 104, 128, 129; and
comparability guide, 106
American Civil Liberties Union, 106
American Council on Education, 205, 207, 212
AFL-CIO, 26
American Federation of Teachers, 21, 208
Anacostia Community School project, Washington, D.C., 120–23
Anguilla, Sharkey County, Miss., 104
Anti-poverty strategy, 11, 61–62. See
also War on poverty
Atlanta, Ga., 42, 46

"Black curriculum," 101
Bloom, Benjamin, 43
Boston, Mass., 122
Brademas, John, Congressman, 207

Briggs, Paul, Cleveland Superintendent, 87
Brown v. Board of Education, 73, 74
Budget, Bureau of the, 35, 36, 48, 72,
115–16

California, 19, 47, 56, 70, 80, 86, 90,
91, 92, 191, 197
Carnegie Commission on Higher Education, 205
Career Opportunities Program, 113
Census, Bureau of the, 161
Change advocates: Title I and, 33,
38–40; within USOE, 35; at state
level, 40, 62, 80
Chicago, Ill., 46, 62, 122, 197; and
Title I funds, 63–65
Chicago Coordinating Council of
Community Organization, 63
Chief state school officers, 36, 46, 62,
125; Council of, 73
Child benefit formula, 12, 18, 20
Child Development, Office of,
DHEW, 219
CRA (Civil Rights Act), 7, 12, 34,
42, 58, 61, 109, 135, 138, 156, 202;
Title VI, 42, 63–64, 73–75, 139
Civil rights groups, 117
Cleveland, Ohio, 86–88, 94, 95; ladder of program services, 88; Reading Improvement Project, 88–90;
concentration model, 90, 93
Client advocacy movement, 107, 108,
109, 124; and opportunity strategy,
110; and public schools, 110–11,